being a great
America͢n!
J A

INTERVIEWS WITH THE FOUNDERS

THE WAY AMERICA IS NOW - AND THE WAY AMERICA IS SUPPOSED TO BE

JUSTIN AMERICAN

Published by Justinamerican.com
ISBN-13: 978-0692303450
ISBN-10: 0692303456

First, Americans fought for their own freedom...

---

1   The Death of General Warren at Bunker Hill, by John Trumbell
2   Washington and French General Rochambeau give orders at Yorktown

TABLE OF INTERVIEWS

PROLOGUE

From May 1831 to Feb 1832, a French Aristocrat, Alexis de Tocqueville, toured the USA, then less than 50 years old. France supposedly sent him to study the US prison system, but Tocqueville did an extensive study of the whole of American society. The quote below comes from chapter 6, "What Sort of Despotism Democratic Nations Have to Fear," of *Democracy In America*, volume II, part 4.

"I seek to trace the novel features under which despotism may appear in the world. The first thing that strikes the observation is an innumerable multitude of men all equal and alike, incessantly endeavoring to procure the petty and paltry pleasures with which they glut their lives. Each of them, living apart, is as a stranger to the fate of all the rest—his children and his private friends constitute to him the whole of mankind; as for the rest of his fellow-citizens, he is close to them, but he sees them not—he touches them, but he feels them not; he exists but in himself and for himself alone; and if his kindred still remain to him, he may be said at any rate to have lost his country. Above this race of men stands an immense and tutelary power [the government], which takes upon itself alone to secure their gratifications, and to watch over their fate. That power is absolute, minute, regular, provident, and mild. It would be like the authority of a parent, if, like that authority, its object was to prepare men for manhood; but it seeks on the contrary to keep them in perpetual childhood: it is well content that the people should rejoice, provided they think of nothing but rejoicing. For their happiness such a government willingly labors, but it chooses to be the sole agent and the only arbiter of that happiness: it provides for their security, foresees and supplies their necessities, facilitates their pleasures, manages their principal concerns, directs their industry, regulates the descent of property, and subdivides their inheritances—what remains, but to spare them all the care of thinking and all the trouble of living? Thus it every day renders the exercise of the free agency of man less useful and less frequent; it circumscribes the will within a narrower range, and gradually robs a man of all the uses of himself. The principle of equality has prepared men for these things: it has predisposed men to endure them, and oftentimes to look on them as benefits.

After having thus successively taken each member of the community in its powerful grasp, and fashioned them at will, the supreme power [the government] then extends its arm over the whole community. It covers the surface of society with a network of small complicated rules, minute and uniform, through which the most original minds and the most energetic characters cannot penetrate, to rise above the crowd. The will of man is not shattered, but softened, bent, and guided: men are seldom forced by it to act, but they are constantly restrained from acting: such a power does not destroy, but it prevents existence; it does not tyrannize, but it compresses, enervates, extinguishes, and stupefies a people, until each nation is reduced to be nothing better than a flock of timid and industrious animals, of which the government is the shepherd."

Alexis de Tocqueville, from his book about his travels in the USA, *Democracy in America*, (public domain copy from www.Gutenberg.org)

I ask you, my fellow Americans, here in 2014, has Tocqueville's prediction come true in modern day America? Given the size and scope of the federal government, which regulates everything from the sale of milk (21 CFR Sec. 1240.61), to the building of a fishing/swimming pond on a farm ($75,000/day fine if you are not in compliance with EPA rules), to threatening multi-thousand dollar per day fines for oil field workers in Kansas if they unduly disturb the local lesser prairie chicken population, to a 2,000 page law that is so big that Congress has to "pass the bill so that you can find out what is in it," have we become "a flock of timid and industrious animals, of which the government is the shepherd?"

If, after reading this book, you believe that we have become American sheep, I challenge you to cut off the wool that has enveloped you in a cocoon of comfortable bliss about the state of your nation, and to "rise above the crowd" – to become a lion for life, liberty, and the pursuit of happiness.

Read this next quote closely, maybe even twice. Ponder it for a minute or two and really make sure you digest its gist.

"Experience should teach us to be most on our guard to protect liberty when the government's purposes are beneficent. Men born to freedom are naturally alert to repel invasion of their liberty by evil-minded rulers. The greatest dangers to liberty lurk in insidious encroachment by men of zeal, well-meaning but without understanding."

Louis Brandeis, United States Supreme Court Justice, 1928

Ladies and Gents – we owe it to ourselves, to our kids, to our grandkids, and to posterity – to ensure that we do not put people in public office who are "well-meaning but without understanding."

To fix America's problems, we must elect leaders who first understand the way America is now, and who then bring us back around to the way America is supposed to be.

Your humble servant
Justin American

FOREWORD

What would the Founding Fathers say about America today?

Friends, Americans, countrymen-lend me your ears. I originally intended for this book to be added to the copious annals of the lengthy and mostly boring historical works on the founding of the USA. Thankfully, for you the reader and for me, I had a moment of inspiration, and what I present to you now is a compilation of, via the form of an interview, the exact words of the Founding Fathers as they relate to America's establishment and its current state of affairs.

When I say "exact words," I mean that almost literally. This book will use quotations from the Founding Fathers and a few other prominent Americans as responses to questions that I, the interview moderator, will pose. I have only made two types of changes to the quotations. First, if I felt the original language was difficult to comprehend for the modern reader, I modified obsolete or obscure words and phrases with more modern equivalents. Second, in order to make the interview flow in a more conversational manner, I have added words preceding, between, and after quotations that do not alter the quotations' meaning. All the Founders' quotations will be within quotation marks. The symbols [] are the standard way of adding words for clarification within a quotation. Additionally, I have used due diligence in trying to assure that these quotes do come from a reputable, original source, but citing each individual quote and its source would make the book too lengthy and cumbersome. This book is not meant to be an academic research document. Rather, it is more like a journalistic interview. I've clearly indicated the people I am quoting, and if you really want to find a quote's source, just copy and paste a few words of the quote, with the name of the person who said it, into an Internet search engine, and your itch will be quickly scratched.

Additionally, I will spare you the long introductory explanation that most authors put at the front of their books to tell the readers what the book is going to tell them before they read the book – where's the fun in that?

The Founding Fathers and other great Americans can speak for themselves, and their ideas become clear if one merely takes the time to listen to what they have to say. So, without further ado, we will let them speak, to remind us "modern" Americans of their brilliance, foresight, and courage as they struggled, by the pen and by the sword, to establish America with life, liberty, and the pursuit of happiness.

I pose the following question for reflection as we revive the words of wisdom from our greatest Americans: if we are not happy with the current state of American affairs, might it be because we have deviated – indeed wholly ignored in many cases – the sage advice of those Americans who, often at great personal hardship, sacrifice, and even loss of life, founded and preserved the union of the United States of America, to ensure that "government of the people, by the people, for the people shall not perish from the earth?"

Justin American

A note for you Founding Father skeptics – ye without sin, cast the first stone! Yes, some of the Founders owned slaves. However, we need to focus on the political, economic, and social system that these collective learned minds developed – not the fact they, being fallible human beings like us, did not always live up to their wise ideals.

Acknowledgments:

First and foremost, I acknowledge the support and encouragement of my wife during the time that I worked on this book. I took that time from our marriage, and she graciously made that sacrifice to allow me to accomplish my goals in this book.

And thanks to my friends for your encouragement – you know who I am, and I know who you are. Additionally, I thank my bright son for the time he spent editing my draft for readability.

The Founding Father quotes in this book come from a variety of sources: books of quotations, websites with quotes, etc.

I acknowledge The Gutenberg Project as a source of quotes in this book, and this book contains only uncopyrighted Gutenberg Project material. Also, I acknowledge Wikiquote, with quotations used by permission under the creative commons license -
http://creativecommons.org/licenses/by-sa/3.0/legalcode.

However, to ensure the quotes' authenticity, I confirmed their source via reference to original documents. To this end, I gratefully acknowledge the Lillian Goldman Law Library for their extensive online collection of colonial period documents. Additionally, I thank the American National Historical Publications and Records Commission for hosting the website *founders.archives.gov*. Close to 150,000 documents from the Founding Fathers and other early American historical figures have been transcribed and put on this government website for public use. All Americans should thank The University of Virginia, Princeton University, the Massachusetts Historical Society, Columbia University, Yale University, the American Philosophical Society, the University of Chicago, and the Thomas Jefferson Foundation at Monticello for their contributions to *founders.archives. gov*. Check out *founders.archives.gov*, and if you believe that this website has value, don't hesitate to make a contribution to the organizations mentioned above to recognize their efforts.

A quick note on author's bias: I am a devout Christian and politically conservative. But, I have made a sincere effort to be non-partisan and to "call'em like I see'em" as regards the political, social, religious, and financial views of the Founding Fathers. For instance, I'd like to believe that all the Founding Fathers were devout, evangelical Christians.

But such is not the case, and I acknowledge this fact in the religious interview. Additionally, though generally pro-military, I do point out the dangers of excessive military spending and the collusion of the military-industrial complex, as pointed out by George Washington.

Finally, while political, social, and religious hot potatoes will be discussed, this book does not support any particular political party or politician. I let the Founding Fathers' words speak for themselves, and then I endeavor to let the chips fall where they may. Left, Right, and Center will find ample material herein to support their ideologies - and to make them cringe with embarrassment when they see how out of touch they are with the Founding Fathers' vision for the USA.

CHAPTER 1

PLEASANTRIES AND INTRODUCTIONS

Justin American/Moderator (MOD): Good afternoon Gentlemen. I'm humbled and honored by the opportunity to converse with such a group of eminent Americans. Before we get started, I will take a moment to remind our audience of the composition of today's distinguished panel.

The Honorable President George Washington (GW) served as the first president of the USA, serving two terms from 1789-1797. Though having only the equivalent of an elementary education, Washington progressed from the ranks of land surveyor to become an officer in the Virginia militia and a member of the Virginia state legislature, subsequently being nominated by the Second Continental Congress as Commander-in-Chief of the Continental Army during the Revolutionary War. Washington did own slaves, but he became increasingly against slavery during his lifetime, and his will provided for the freeing of his slaves upon the death of his widow.

The Honorable John Adams (JA) was the second president of the USA. He was a highly educated man holding a BA from Harvard and a law degree from Worcester College. He represented Massachusetts at the First Continental Congress, participated with Thomas Jefferson on the development of the Declaration of Independence, and wrote prolifically throughout most of his life in support of American independence. He represented the USA diplomatically in France, Holland, and Britain. John Adams was also America's first Vice-President. John Adams did not, apparently, own any slaves, and the Massachusetts State Constitution, authored primarily by Adams, forbade slavery.

The Honorable Thomas Jefferson (TJ) served two terms as the third American president from 1801-1809. Jefferson, a Virginian like Washington, attended the College of William and Mary, studying a variety of subjects such as mathematics, metaphysics, philosophy, and political science. He read and studied in both Greek and French, and played the violin. After practicing law for a number of years, Jefferson became a member of the Virginia legislative assembly, the House of Burgesses, and was a Virginian delegate to the Second Continental Congress in June 1775. Returning to Virginia, he was elected Governor of Virginia in 1779. In 1783, Jefferson became a member of the Continental Congress, and he served as the American Minister to France from 1785-1789. In Sept 1789, he became Secretary of State and served as Vice President of the USA from 1797-1801, finally becoming the third American President in 1801.[3] Jefferson was the primary author of the Declaration of Independence.

The Honorable James Madison (JM) succeeded Thomas Jefferson and served two terms as the fourth President of the USA from 1809-1817. A Virginian by birth, Madison attended the College of New Jersey (now Princeton University), and studied a variety of subjects such as mathematics, rhetoric, philosophy, Latin, Hebrew, and Greek. Madison twice served in the Virginia state legislature, before and after the American Revolutionary War. An early champion of religious freedom, he and Jefferson helped write the Virginia Statute for Religious Freedom. Madison also served as a member of the Continental Congress from 1780-1783, and he became a member of the Virginia delegation at the Constitutional Convention in 1787. Madison's Virginia Plan became the starting point for the Convention's work, leading to his moniker "Father of the Constitution." Madison wrote a number of the 85 *Federalist Papers*, possibly as many as 26, and these documents were instrumental

---

[3]   Thomas Jefferson and John Adams died on the same day – July 4th, 1826 – Divine intervention? I report, you decide.

in securing ratification of the Constitution. Madison then served as a member of Congress, Jefferson's Secretary of State, and became the fourth American President.

The Honorable Benjamin Franklin (BF) was a diplomat, scientist, inventor, and legislator, among his other various talents and occupations. With very little early education and no college degree, Franklin nonetheless read copiously and educated himself on everything from physics to political science. Franklin served in many public positions: member of the Pennsylvania Assembly, Pennsylvania's Colonial Representative to Great Britain, member of the Second Continental Congress, America's first Postmaster General, Ambassador to France, a Pennsylvania Representative to the Constitutional Convention, and President of the Supreme Executive Council of Pennsylvania (essentially the Governor).

The Honorable Alexander Hamilton (AH) was the first American Secretary of the Treasury under President Washington. Born and raised in the West Indies, he moved to Boston, Massachusetts, in 1772, studied at a college preparatory school, and then enrolled at King's College, NY, (now Columbia University). In 1775, Hamilton joined the revolutionary cause as a member of the New York militia, rose quickly through the ranks, and became General Washington's Chief of Staff. At the end of the Revolutionary War, Hamilton became a member of New York's delegation to the Continental Congress. An ardent proponent of the Constitution, historians estimate that he wrote 51 of *The Federalist Papers*. Washington appointed Hamilton as the first Secretary of the Treasury, and Hamilton was instrumental in developing an American banking system that could put the brand new USA on firm financial footing. Hamilton returned to private law practice in 1795 and finished out his days in this capacity, while still having significant influence in New York state and national politics.[4]

---

[4]   Then Vice-President Aaron Burr challenged Hamilton to a duel, accusing Hamilton of playing a significant role in Burr's defeat during the New York gubernatorial election of 1804. On 12 Jul 1804, Burr shot and killed Hamilton during the duel.

CHAPTER 2

POLITICAL PARTY STALEMATE

"In all political societies, different interests and parties arise out of the nature of things, and the great art of politicians lies in making them checks and balances to each other." James Madison

MOD: Gentlemen, you have graciously agreed to join me today to address the current state of affairs in the American Republic that you all cherished so deeply. Today, in 2014, 225 years after the implementation of the American Constitution on March 4th, 1789, the USA has become the economic, military, and some would even say cultural superpower of the world. And yet, the country faces great crises of enormous national debt, political gridlock, social and religious tensions, and interminable wars abroad. These crises have been long in the making, and the blame can be equally divided on both sides of a political spectrum that has become virtually a two party system, Republicans and Democrats. Gentlemen – let's start right there - what say you about a narrowly limited political party system? President Washington, as the first among equals on this panel, I give you the podium to begin our discussions.

GW: Before making any remarks, please allow me a few brief comments on today's discussions. We, the Founding Fathers, gave to our posterity a system of government and a Judeo-Christian ethic – but not religion - that were intended to be guideposts for the future of the country. I hope that today's discussions will provide some insight to current and future generations on how the USA was supposed to be governed and how it is governed today.

And, there's no better place to start our discourse than with the intrigues of the current two party system. "The alternate domination of one faction [party] over another, sharpened by the spirit of revenge, natural to party dissension, which in different ages and countries has perpetrated the most horrid evils, is itself a frightful tyranny. But this leads at length to a more formal and permanent despotism. The disorders and miseries, which result, gradually incline the minds of men to seek security and repose in the absolute power of an individual; and sooner or later the chief of some prevailing faction, more able or more fortunate than his competitors, turns this disposition to the purposes of his own elevation, on the ruins of public liberty."

"The common and continual mischiefs of the spirit of party are sufficient to make it the interest and duty of a wise people to discourage and restrain it. It serves always to distract the public councils and weaken the public administration. It agitates the community with ill-founded jealousies and false alarms; kindles the animosity of one part against another, and foments occasionally riot and insurrection."

MOD: Very well said Sir - I remember this admonishment in your farewell address about the excesses of political parties, and…

JM: If I may, I would like to echo and expound on the President's comments. If I might recall a bit of "Federalist Paper 10" that I wrote, in my time and in modern times, we are seeing an "increasing distrust of public engagements, and alarm for private rights, which are echoed from one end of the continent to the other. These must be chiefly, if not wholly, effects of the unsteadiness and injustice with which a factious [party] spirit has tainted our public administrations."

MOD: So, with the current President's approval rating well under 50% and Congress's approval rating hovering around 20%, it appears, President Madison, that you might be blaming factions - what we might call modern day political parties - for our current distrust of our public servants and for Americans' anxiety about an ever expanding government taking more and more of their rights, liberty, and property?

JM: Oh most definitely. "By a faction, I understand a number of citizens, whether amounting to a majority or a minority of the whole, who are united and activated by some common impulse of passion, or of interest, adverse to the rights of other citizens, or to the permanent and total interests of the community. The diversity in the talents of men, from which the rights of property originate, is definitely an insurmountable obstacle to a uniformity of interests [equality of outcomes]. The protection of these talents is the first object of government. From the protection of different and unequal talents of acquiring property, the possession of different degrees and kinds of property immediately results; and from the influence of these on the sentiments and views of the respective proprietors, follows a division of the society into different interests and parties.

The hidden causes of faction are thus sown in the nature of man; and we see them everywhere brought into different degrees of activity, according to the different circumstances of civil society. A zeal for different opinions concerning religion, concerning government, and many other points, as well of speculation as of practice; an attachment to different leaders ambitiously contending for pre-eminence and power; or to persons of other descriptions whose fortunes have been interesting to the human passions, have, in turn, divided mankind into parties, inflamed them with mutual animosity, and rendered them much more disposed to vex and oppress each other than to co-operate for their common good. "

MOD: Hmmm – well, President Madison, your words are certainly clairvoyant. The USA has experienced 18 full or partial government shutdowns over the last 40 years or so, depriving millions of Americans of billions of dollars in lost wages, causing many Americans to lose their jobs, all while the politicians keep their jobs and their salaries and benefits.

JM: Yes, I guess, sadly, I was right when I said that political factions tend to divide "mankind into parties, inflamed…with mutual animosity, and rendered…much more disposed to vex and oppress each other than to co-operate for their common good."

MOD: Would anyone else like to comment on the subject of political parties?

TJ: Yes, if I might be permitted a few words on the subject. First, let me make a general statement about politics: "If we do not learn to sacrifice small differences of opinion, we can never act together. Every man cannot have his way in all things. If his own opinion prevails at some times, he should acquiesce on seeing that of others preponderate at others. Without this mutual disposition we are disjointed individuals, but not a society."

That being said, "The greatest good we can do our country is to heal its party divisions and make them one people. I do not speak of their leaders who are incurable, but of the honest and well-intentioned body of the people."

Personally, "I never submitted the whole system of my opinions to the creed of any party of men whatever in religion, in philosophy, in politics, or in anything else where I was capable of thinking for myself. Such an addiction is the last ruin of a free and moral agent. If I could not go to heaven but with a party, I would not go there at all."

JA: Yes, I would concur with President Jefferson's comments, and I will add that "the essence of a free government consists in an effectual control of rivalries. The nation which will not adopt an equilibrium of power must adopt a despotism. There is no other alternative. Rivalries must be controlled, or they will throw all things into confusion; and there is nothing but despotism or a balance of power which can control them."

"There is nothing which I dread so much as a division of the republic into two great parties, each arranged under its leader, and concerting measures in opposition to each other. This, in my humble apprehension, is to be dreaded as the greatest political evil under our Constitution."

MOD: Secretary Hamilton, thoughts?

AH: I will simply state that "A spirit of faction, which is apt to mingle its poison in the deliberations of all bodies of men, will often hurry the persons of whom they are composed into improprieties and excesses, for which they would blush in a private capacity."

MOD: Since there seems to be general agreement on the evils of factions and political parties in government, let us move on to an issue that might prove a bit more contentious...but wait – I believe we have another distinguished American President who will be joining us. Gentlemen, meet the 16th President of the USA, Abraham Lincoln (AL), who led our divided country through a civil war to preserve the Union and to end slavery. The Civil War clearly shows the danger for a country when it finds itself divided into factions.

TJ: Well, any man who accomplished the feat of ending slavery in the USA deserves a seat at our table, because "can the liberties of a nation be thought secure when we have removed their only firm basis, a conviction in the minds of the people that these liberties are of the gift of God? That they are not to be violated but with his wrath? Indeed, I tremble for my country when I reflect that God is just: that his justice cannot sleep forever."

AL: Well President Jefferson, your words have proved to be ominously true, for I said in the darkest hours of the Civil War, "If God now wills the removal of a great wrong [slavery], and wills also that we of the North as well as you of the South, shall pay fairly for our complicity in that wrong, impartial history will find therein new cause to attest and revere the justice and goodness of God." As the Good Book says, "a house divided against itself cannot stand."[5]

---

[5]   On the 16th of June, 1858, while running for a US Senate seat in Illinois, Abraham Lincoln gave what has come to be known as the "House Divided

MOD: Thank you President Lincoln for those sobering words that confirmed President Jefferson's prediction. Today, in 2014, the USA again finds itself fractured into factions and in grave danger from skyrocketing government debt, excessive government intervention into citizens' lives, and culture wars. Gentlemen, these last comments are a good segue (lead-in) to our next topic.

End of this interview

Key quotes:

"The common and continual mischiefs of the spirit of party are sufficient to make it the interest and duty of a wise people to discourage and restrain it. It serves always to distract the public councils and weaken the public administration. It agitates the community with ill-founded jealousies and false alarms; kindles the animosity of one part against another, and foments occasionally riot and insurrection." Washington

"There is nothing which I dread so much as a division of the republic into two great parties, each arranged under its leader, and concerting measures in opposition to each other. This, in my humble apprehension, is to be dreaded as the greatest political evil under our Constitution." Adams

Moderator's Notes: The 2013 partial government shutdown represented an egregious (very bad) example of party politics. Political leaders who refuse to allow the democratic process to move forward by blocking legislative votes exercise a form of political tyranny totally contrary to American republican, democratic ideals. Washington said it best:

Speech." Lincoln's speech espoused the idea that the USA, divided by slavery into north and south, could not continue to exist. To drive home his point, Lincoln used a biblical reference, "And if a house be divided against itself, that house cannot stand." Lincoln did not choose these words by chance. He knew that Americans of his time would certainly know this Biblical allusion, further bolstering my claim in chapter 4 that American morality and mores are Judeo-Christian based.

"All obstructions to the execution of the Laws, all combinations and associations, under whatever plausible character, with the real design to direct, control, counteract, or awe the regular deliberation and action of the constituted authorities, are destructive of this fundamental principle, and of fatal tendency. They serve to organize faction, to give it an artificial and extraordinary force---to put in the place of the delegated will of the nation, the will of a party, often a small but artful and enterprising minority of the community; and, according to the alternate triumphs of different parties, to make the public administration the mirror of the ill concerted and incongruous projects of faction, rather than the organ of consistent and wholesome plans digested by common councils, and modified by mutual interests."

Whether it's politicians who leave the confines of their state to inhibit a legislative quorum for a vote on a proposed law, or a faction of a political party that refuses to vote to fund the government as a protest to an existing law, or political leaders who refuse to allow proposed legislation to come up for a vote because the legislation is not in line with their political views – all these actions, and the people who do them, are destructive to our political process. The Founders, and especially Washington, would be ashamed of those who block the legislative process and the enactment of justly passed laws! Politicians – make your best arguments, let the votes take place, and let We the People suffer the consequences, good or bad, of the votes we elected you to make.

Note to voters: As of Jan 14, Congressional approval rates were around 15%, depending on the poll consulted. 15%? Wow! That means 85% of Americans don't approve of the work of Congress, yet since the 1980s, voters have re-elected incumbents by at least a 75% margin, and the House of Representatives, since 1964, has had a re-election rate at or above 85%, with many election cycles well above 90%.[6]

---

[6] http://www.huffingtonpost.com/2010/05/26/will-2010-really-be-an-an_n_590434.html

As Marcellus says in <u>Hamlet</u>, "Something is rotten is Denmark." Well, that rottenness is the apathy of many US voters who, though discontented with their elected officials, continue to go to the polls and to pull the lever for the guy/gal already sitting in the seat, apparently forgetting that by an almost a 6 to 1 margin, Americans disapprove of Congress's work.

Fellow Americans – we only have ourselves to blame for this sad state of affairs. And as usual, the Founders and other statesman from America's past warned us about this kind of voter apathy:

"We electors have an important constitutional power placed in our hands: We have a check upon two branches of the legislature, as each branch has upon the other two; the power I mean of electing, at stated periods, one branch, which branch has the power of electing another. It becomes necessary to every subject then, to be in some degree a statesman: and to examine and judge for himself of the tendency of political principles and measures." John Adams

"Nothing is more essential to the establishment of manners in a State than that all persons employed in places of power and trust be men of unexceptionable characters. The public cannot be too curious concerning the character of public men." Samuel Adams, cousin of John Adams

"The elective franchise, if guarded as the ark of our safety, will peaceably dissipate all combinations to subvert a Constitution, dictated by the wisdom, and resting on the will of the people." Jefferson

"Let men be good and the government cannot be bad.... But if men be bad, let the government be never so good, they will endeavor to warp and spoil it to their turn....though good laws do well, good men do better; for good laws may want [lack] good men and be abolished or invaded by ill men; but good men will never want good laws nor suffer [allow] ill ones." Noah Webster

"Now, more than ever before, the people are responsible for the character of their Congress. If that body be ignorant, reckless, and corrupt, it is because the people tolerate ignorance, recklessness, and corruption. If it be intelligent, brave, and pure, it is because the people demand these high qualities to represent them in the national legislature.... If the next centennial does not find us a great nation... it will be because those who represent the enterprise, the culture, and the morality of the nation do not aid in controlling the political forces." -- President James Garfield

And finally – let's hope this gem from Jefferson will once again prove to be true.

"Should things go wrong at any time, the people will set them to rights [set them straight] by the peaceable exercise of their elective rights."

Fellow Americans – now is the time to set things straight!

CHAPTER 3

UNCLE SAM – HOW BIG SHOULD HE BE?

"If men were angels, no government would be necessary. If angels were to govern men, neither external nor internal controls on government would be necessary. In framing a government which is to be administered by men over men, the great difficulty lies in this: You must first enable the government to control the governed; and in the next place, oblige it to control itself." "The Federalist Number 51"

"Power always thinks it has a great soul and vast view beyond the comprehension of the weak; and that it is doing God's service, when it is violating His laws." John Adams

"A government big enough to give you everything you want is a government big enough to take from you everything you have."
38th US President Gerald Ford

MOD: Gentlemen, let us turn our lively discussions to your views on the role, size, and nature of the government created by the American Constitution. For comparison purposes, let me start by pointing out that the staff of the first Secretary of State, Thomas Jefferson, had only seven members: the Secretary of State, a Chief Clerk, three other clerks, a translator, and a messenger, with a total annual budget of $56,600. Today, the Department of State employs nearly 50,000 employees, with an annual budget of over $57 billion in 2012.

President Jefferson, as you were the first Secretary of State, what say you on the subject of the size and role of government?

TJ: I stated in my first inaugural address that a vital premise of government is "economy in the public expense." In my second inaugural address, I directly addressed the issue of public debt, stating that it is "encroaching on the rights of future generations, by burdening them with the debts of the past."

Also, in my first inaugural address, after many years in public service and after having spent many years overseas as a diplomat for the American cause, I told my fellow citizens that "a wise and frugal government, which shall restrain men from injuring one another, shall leave them otherwise free to regulate their own pursuits of industry and improvement, and shall not take from the mouth of labor the bread it has earned. This is the sum of good government; and this is necessary to close the circle of our felicities [happiness]."

MOD: Yes, yes, "frugal" - meaning the avoidance of unnecessary spending of money – the American government is currently in 2014 borrowing about one of every three dollars it spends, accumulating massive amounts of public debt now surpassing 17 trillion dollars, exceeding the current $16 trillion a year American gross domestic economic product, and this sum does not include tens of trillions of dollars in additional debt owed in government entitlement programs. Do you have any further comments President Jefferson?

TJ: I once told James Madison "no generation may contract debts greater than may be paid during its own existence... with respect to future debts, would it not be wise & just for that nation to declare, in the constitution they are forming, that neither the legislature, nor the nation itself, can validly contract more debt than they may pay within their own age?"

I was a champion of cutting government waste, and I pointed out my efforts in my second inaugural address: "The suppression of unnecessary offices, of useless establishments and expenses, enabled us to discontinue our internal taxes. These, covering our land with officers and opening our doors to their intrusions, had already begun that process of domiciliary vexation which once entered is scarcely to be restrained from reaching successively every article of property and produce. If among these taxes some minor ones fell which had not been inconvenient, it was because their amount would not have paid the officers who collected them, and because, if they had any merit, the State authorities might adopt them instead of others less approved."

"The multiplication of public offices, increase of expense beyond income, growth and entailment of a public debt, are indications soliciting the employment of the pruning knife."

"And I sincerely believe...that banking establishments are more dangerous than standing armies; and that the principle of spending money to be paid by posterity in the name of funding, is but swindling futurity on a large scale."

"It is incumbent on every generation to pay its own debts as it goes, a principle which, if acted on, would save one half the wars of the world."

"I, however, place economy among the first and most important republican virtues, and public debt as the greatest of the dangers to be feared."

"We must not let our rulers load us with perpetual debt. *We must make our election between economy and liberty, or profusion and servitude* [emphasis added]."

MOD: Well, President Jefferson, am I correct in stating that you were very concerned about the growth of the federal government because such growth would cause ever increasing public debt and would dangerously increase the power of the federal government to intrude on the domestic lives of American citizens?

TJ: Please allow me to cite from a letter I wrote to Mr. Joseph Cabell that outlines my ideas on the division of state and federal powers: "Let the national government be entrusted with the defense of the nation, and its foreign and federal relations; the State governments with the civil rights, laws, police, and administration of what concerns the State generally; the counties with the local concerns of the counties, and each ward direct the interests within itself. It is by dividing and subdividing these republics from the great national one down through all its subordinations, until it ends in the administration of every man's farm by himself; by placing under everyone what his own eye may superintend, that all will be done for the best."

I expressed further my concerns about an ever growing federal government: "What has destroyed liberty and the rights of man in every government which has ever existed under the sun? The generalizing and concentrating all cares and powers into one body, no matter whether of the autocrats of Russia or France, or of the aristocrats of a Venetian senate."

"Our country is too large to have all its affairs directed by a single government. Public servants at such a distance, and from under the eye of their constituents, must, from the circumstance of distance, be unable to administer and overlook all the details necessary for the good government of the citizens; and the same circumstance, by rendering detection impossible to their constituents, will invite public agents to corruption, plunder and waste."

"Were we directed from Washington when to sow, & when to reap, we should soon want bread. It is by this partition of cares, descending in gradation from general to particular, that the mass of human affairs may be best managed for the good and prosperity of all."

...Finally, near the end of my natural life, I restated my position on the role of the federal government in my 1825 "Draft Declaration and Protest of the Commonwealth of Virginia, on the Principles of the Constitution of the United States of America, and on the Violations of them" when I wrote that one of the greatest calamities that could befall the USA would be "submission to a government of unlimited powers."

MOD: It appears that you are against the consolidation of more and more power in the federal government?

TJ: Oh yes, most definitely because "it is not by the consolidation or concentration of powers, but by their distribution that good government is effected. Were not this great country already divided into States, that division must be made that each might do for itself what concerns itself directly and what it can so much better do than a distant authority. Every state again is divided into counties, each to take care of what lies within its local bounds; each county again into townships or wards, to manage more minute details; and every ward into farms, to be governed each by its individual proprietor."

"The functionaries of every government have propensities to command at will the liberty and property of their constituents."

Should we "commit to the governor and council the management of all our farms, our mills and merchants' stores? No, my friend, the way to have good and safe government is not to trust it all to one, but to divide it among the many, distributing to every one exactly the functions he is competent to. One method of assault may be to effect in the forms of the Constitution alterations which will impair the energy of the system, and thus to undermine what cannot be directly overthrown... Liberty itself will find in such a government, with powers properly distributed and adjusted, its surest guardian."

MOD: President Jefferson, thank you for your most enlightening comments. President Washington, I seem to remember that you too were very concerned about the unconstitutional consolidation of governmental powers. In recent times, Presidents of all parties have been prone to use more and more executive power to put in place federal regulations that they cannot get passed by the Congress as laws. What do you think of such practices?

GW: "It is important...that the habits of thinking in a free country, should inspire caution, in those entrusted with its administration, to confine themselves within their respective constitutional spheres, avoiding in the exercise of the powers of one department to encroach upon another. The spirit of encroachment tends to consolidate the powers of all the departments in one, and thus to create, whatever the form of government, a real despotism...If, in the opinion of the People, the distribution or modification of the constitutional powers be in any particular wrong, let it be corrected by an amendment in the way which the constitution designates.—*But let there be no change by usurpation; for though this, in one instance, may be the instrument of good, it is the customary weapon by which free governments are destroyed.—The precedent must always greatly overbalance in permanent evil any partial or transient benefit which the use can at any time yield* [emphasis added]."

MOD: But what about the "General Welfare" clause of the Constitution? Does the preamble to the Constitution not say that "We the people" empower the government to look after the "general welfare" of the nation?

JM: "If Congress can do whatever in their discretion can be done by money, and will promote the general welfare, the Government is no longer a limited one possessing enumerated powers, but an indefinite one subject to particular exceptions. *It is to be remarked that the phrase out of which this doctrine is elaborated, is copied from the old Articles of Confederation, where it was always understood as nothing more than a general caption to the specified powers, and it is a fact that it was preferred in the new instrument [Constitution] for that very reason as less liable than any other to misunderstanding* [emphasis added]."

"If Congress can apply money indefinitely to the general welfare, and are the sole and supreme judges of the general welfare, they may take the care of religion into their own hands; they may establish teachers in every State, county, and parish, and pay them out of the public Treasury; they may take into their own hands the education of children, establishing in like manner schools throughout the Union; they may undertake the regulation of all roads other than post roads. In short, everything, from the highest object of State legislation, down to the most minute object of police, would be thrown under the power of Congress; for every object I have mentioned would admit the application of money, and might be called, if Congress pleased, provisions for the general welfare."

MOD: So it appears that you agree with President Jefferson that care should be taken in order that the federal government not be allowed to interfere with affairs that are not part of its enumerated powers?

JM: Oh, most definitely yes! "The government of the United States is a definite government, confined to specified objects. It is not like the state governments, whose powers are more general." Madison

President Jefferson, did you not say "Our tenet ever was...that Congress had not unlimited powers to provide for the general welfare, but were restrained to those specifically enumerated; and that, as it was never meant they should provide for that welfare but by the exercise of the enumerated powers, so it could not have been meant they should raise money for purposes which the enumeration did not place under their action; consequently, that the specification of powers is a limitation of the purposes for which they may raise money."

TJ: I did indeed write those exact words to Mr. Albert Gallatin in 1817, concerning a presidential veto of proposed federal legislation.

And in 1825, I told my acquaintance Mr. William Giles that "I see as you do, and with the deepest affliction, the rapid strides with which the federal branch of our government is advancing towards the usurpation of all the rights reserved to the states, and the consolidation in itself of all powers foreign and domestic; and that too by constructions which, if legitimate, leave no limits to their power, take together the decisions of the federal court, the doctrines of the President, and the misconstructions of the constitutional compact, acted on by the legislature of the federal branch and it is but too evident that the three ruling branches of that department are in combination to strip their Colleagues, the States authorities, of the powers reserved by them and to exercise themselves all functions foreign and domestic."

MOD: Well, I can tell you Sir that things have only gotten worse concerning the diminishment of states' rights.

TJ: How can we make this point any clearer on our insistence that the federal government be limited to its enumerated, constitutional powers? Congress is not supposed to "lay taxes...*for any purpose they please* but only to pay the debts *or provide for the welfare of the Union.* In like manner they are not *to do anything they please* to provide for the general welfare, but only *to lay taxes* for that purpose. To consider the latter phrase, not as describing the purpose of the first, but as giving a distinct & independent power to do any act they please, which might be for the good of the Union, would render all the preceding & subsequent enumerations of power completely useless. It would reduce the whole instrument to a single phrase, that of instituting a Congress with power to do whatever would be for the good of the U.S. and as they would be the sole judges of the good or evil, it would be also a power to do whatever evil they pleased." I would even go so far as to say "that whensoever the general government assumes undelegated powers, its acts are unauthoritative, void, and of no force...that the government created by this compact was not made the exclusive or final judge of the extent of the powers delegated to itself; since that would have made its discretion, and not the Constitution, the measure of its powers."

JM: I must chime in again, for I too sternly warned about the slow, yet steady, taking of more and more power by federal officials: "Since the general civilization of mankind, I believe there are more instances of the abridgment of the freedom of the people, by gradual and silent encroachments of those in power, than by violent and sudden usurpations."

Americans must "hold the Union of the States as the basis of their peace and happiness; to support the Constitution, which is the cement of the Union, as well in its limitations as in its authorities; to respect the rights and authorities reserved to the States and to the people, as equally incorporated with, and essential to the success of, the general system."

By the way, as regards government's limitations and authorities, I assert that "charity is no part of the legislative duty of the [federal] government."

MOD: No public charity from the government?

JM: I did not say "no governmental public charity." I said that this responsibility is not a delegated federal power, as I am unable "to lay my finger on that article of the Constitution which granted a right to Congress of expending, on objects of benevolence, the money of their constituents."

BF: I would like to add a few comments on public charity. "The good particular men may do separately, in relieving the sick, is small, compared with what they may do collectively." I supported public charity at the state level in the great state of Pennsylvania, going so far as to support the use of public *state* funds, partnered with private funds, for a public hospital because I believed that "the increase of poor diseased foreigners and others, settled in the distant parts of this province, where regular advice and assistance cannot be procured, but at an expense that neither they [the sick and poor] nor their townships can afford, has awakened the attention of diverse humane and well-disposed minds, to procure some more certain, effectual and easy methods for their relief than have hitherto been provided... This branch of charity seems essential to the true spirit of Christianity, and should be extended to all in general, whether deserving or undeserving, as far as our power reaches." But, I never advocated for a nationalized healthcare system – my comments were confined to one public hospital in the state of Pennsylvania, and even that was a public/private partnership where the funding was shared equally by private donations combined with government funds.

MOD: But Mr. Franklin, I believe you said that "All the property that is necessary to a man, for the conservation of the individual and the propagation of the species, is his natural right, which none can justly deprive him of: But all property superfluous to such purposes is the property of the public, who, by their laws, have created it, and who may therefore by other laws dispose of it, whenever the welfare of the public shall demand such disposition. He that does not like civil society on these terms, let him retire and live among savages. He can have no right to the benefits of society, who will not pay his club towards the support of it."

Such a statement certainly could be construed as an endorsement for government to take citizens' excess property – though who gets to determine "excess" is a dubious question – as "the welfare of the public shall demand such disposition." Are you here advocating for national welfare programs?

BF: Sir – you have taken that quote out of context. As for national programs of public charity, I'm inclined to agree with President

Madison's previous comments. I, "for my own part, I am not so well satisfied of the goodness of this thing [taxing citizens to redistribute money to the poor]. I am for doing good to the poor, but I differ in opinion of the means. I think the best way of doing good to the poor, is not making them easy in poverty, but leading or driving them out of it. In my youth I travelled much, and I observed in different countries, that the more public provisions were made for the poor, the less they provided for themselves, and of course became poorer. And, on the contrary, the less was done for them, the more they did for themselves, and became richer. There is no country in the world [England in 1766] where so many provisions are established for them [the poor]; so many hospitals to receive them when they are sick or lame, founded and maintained by voluntary charities; so many alms-houses for the aged of both sexes, together with a solemn general law made by the rich to subject their estates to a heavy tax for the support of the poor. Under all these obligations, are our poor modest, humble, and thankful; and do they use their best endeavors to maintain themselves, and lighten our shoulders of this burden? On the contrary, I affirm that there is no country in the world in which the poor are more idle, dissolute, drunken, and insolent. The day you [English Parliament] passed that act [to tax the rich and give their money to the poor], you took away from before their [the poor's] eyes the greatest of all inducements to industry, frugality, and sobriety, by giving them a dependence on something else than a careful accumulation during youth and health, for support in age or sickness. In short, you offered a premium for the encouragement of idleness, and you should not now wonder that it has had its effect in the increase of poverty. Repeal that law, and you will soon see a change in their manners. St. Monday, and St. Tuesday, will cease to be holidays. Six days shalt thou labor, though one of the old commandments long treated as out of date, will again be looked upon as a respectable precept; industry will increase, and with it plenty among the lower people; their circumstances will mend, and more will be done for their happiness by habituating them to provide for themselves, than could be done by dividing all your estates among them."

TJ: Mr. Franklin, your wisdom rings true to my ear, and I concur wholeheartedly.

"It is while we are young that the habit of industry is formed. If not then, it never is afterwards. The fortune of our lives therefore depends on employing well the short period of youth."

BF: I second those thoughts. To all of my fellow citizens, I advise them to "be studious in your profession, and you will be learned. Be industrious and frugal, and you will be rich. Be sober and temperate and you will be healthy. Be in general virtuous, and you will be happy. At least you will by such conduct stand the best chance for such consequences."

MOD: Gentlemen, in the vein of this topic of public charity and the general welfare, some well-intentioned people have asserted that "equality" means that the government should endeavor to provide an equal distribution of the resources of society to all its citizens? What say you?

JM: Absolutely not! Those who make such assertions have obviously not read "Federalist Paper #10" where I, as previously mentioned, clearly refuted such nonsense: "The diversity in the faculties of men, from which the rights of property originate, is an unsolvable obstacle to an equal distribution of property. The protection of these faculties is the first object of government. From the protection of different and unequal faculties of acquiring property, the possession of different degrees and kinds of property immediately results."

TJ: I am in agreement with President Madison. The government could never, and should never, attempt to make all persons equal in property. "To take from one, because it is thought his own industry and that of his fathers has acquired too much, in order to spare to others, who, or whose fathers, have not exercised equal industry and skill, is to violate arbitrarily the first principle of association, the guarantee to everyone the free exercise of his industry and the fruits acquired by it. If the overgrown wealth of an individual be deemed dangerous to the State, the best corrective is the law of equal inheritance to all in equal degree;

and the better, as this enforces a law of nature, while extra-taxation violates it."[7]

As for equality among citizens, I believe that "equality of rights [be] maintained" as well as "that state of property, equal or unequal, which results to every man from his own industry or that of his father's."

JA: I must chime in here, because in writings defending the American Constitution, I stated that "The moment the idea is admitted into society that property is not as sacred as the laws of God, and that there is not a force of law and public justice to protect it, anarchy and tyranny commence. If 'Thou shalt not covet' and 'Thou shalt not steal' were not commandments of Heaven, they must be made inviolable precepts in every society before it can be civilized or made free."

MOD: Well Gentlemen, your comments seem to be all in favor of not taxing the prosperous to redistribute their property to the less prosperous - thank you for your sage words of counsel. But I would like to bring us back around to the subject at hand: the size and scope of the federal government and its federal expenditures. Are there any further comments on these matters?

GW: While I have previously warned against the federal government being allowed to exceed its enumerated constitutional powers, I would like to now assert my strong aversion to public debt, reaffirming President Jefferson's admonitions in this area. "As a very important source of strength and security, cherish public credit. One method of preserving it is to use it as sparingly as possible; avoiding occasions of expense by cultivating peace, but remembering also that timely disbursements to prepare for danger frequently prevent much greater disbursements to repel it; avoiding likewise the accumulation of debt, not only by shunning occasions of expense, but by vigorous exertions in time of peace to discharge the debts which unavoidable wars may have occasioned, not ungenerously throwing upon posterity the burden which we ourselves ought to bear. The execution of these maxims belongs to

---

[7]   The origin of this quote can be found here: http://www.founding.com/
       founders_library/pageID.2190/default.asp

elected representatives, but it is necessary that public opinion should cooperate."

AH: I was a strong advocate of the necessity of some federal, public debt, but only under the condition that "a national debt, if it is not excessive, will be to us a national blessing."

MOD: Would you agree that a national debt that exceeds the country's annual gross domestic economic product is "excessive?"

AH: I will let my words speak for themselves.

MOD: President Washington, you mentioned defense spending in your recent comments. In constant fiscal year 2001 dollars, military baseline spending (since FY2001), not accounting for overseas contingency operations, has risen by close to 40% in FY 2013. You just stated that it is prudent in times of peace to discharge public debt, but you also stated that we should prepare our armed forces with some expenditures during times of peace to avoid larger expenditures that might be occasioned by unwanted wars. Before you comment on this subject, I'd like to quote from another military leader turned President, Dwight Eisenhower, on the issue of defense spending. "Now this conjunction of an immense military establishment and a large arms industry is new in the American experience. The total influence — economic, political, even spiritual — is felt in every city, every Statehouse, every office of the federal government. We recognize the imperative need for this development. Yet we must not fail to comprehend its grave implications. Our toil, resources, and livelihood are all involved. So is the very structure of our society. In the councils of government, we must guard against the acquisition of unwarranted influence, whether sought or unsought, by the military-industrial complex. The potential for the disastrous rise of misplaced power exists and will persist. We must never let the weight of this combination endanger our liberties or democratic processes. We should take nothing for granted. Only an alert and knowledgeable citizenry can compel the proper meshing of the huge industrial and military machinery of defense with our peaceful methods and goals, so that security and liberty may prosper together."

GW: Very interesting – I will flatter myself just for a moment by reminding us all that I predicted and warned of this problem in 1796, when I counseled my fellow citizens to "avoid the necessity of those overgrown military establishments, which under any form of government are inauspicious to liberty, and which are to be regarded as particularly hostile to Republican Liberty; In this sense it is, that your Union ought to be considered as a main prop of your liberty, and that the love of the one ought to endear to you the preservation of the other."

MOD: A wise king once said "there is nothing new under the sun."

AH: And yet, let me remind my colleagues of the necessity for a strong national defense, as I eloquently stated in *Federalist Paper 23*: "Whether there ought to be a federal government entrusted with the care of the common defense, is a question in the first instance, open for discussion; but the moment it is decided in the affirmative, it will follow, that that government ought to be clothed with all the powers requisite to complete execution of its trust."

GW: I do concur to some degree with Secretary Hamilton, so let me not be misconstrued. I supported a national defense capable of defending the nation against the threat of war. "To be prepared for war is one of the most effectual means of preserving peace." Remember, "there is a rank due to the United States among nations which will be withheld, if not absolutely lost, by the reputation of weakness. If we desire to avoid insult, we must be able to repel it; if we desire to secure peace, one of the most powerful instruments of our rising prosperity, it must be known that we are at all times ready for war."

I favored the establishment of a military academy, firmly believing that "however pacific the general policy of a nation may be, it ought never to be without an adequate stock of military knowledge for emergencies…Whatever argument may be drawn from particular examples, superficially viewed; a thorough examination of the subject will show, that the art of war is at once comprehensive and complicated; that it demands much previous study; and that, the possession of it, in its most improved and perfect state, is always of great moment to the security of a nation. This, therefore, ought to be a serious care of every government; and for this purpose, an academy, where a regular course of instruction is given, is an obvious expedient, which different nations have successfully employed."

JM: Though I supported "economy in public expenditures; to liberate the public resources by an honorable discharge of the public debts," I also advised that the US "keep within the requisite limits a standing military force, always remembering, that an armed and trained militia is the firmest bulwark [safeguard] of Republics."

TJ: I'd like to comment, please. I once said that "the spirit of this country is totally adverse to a large military force."

However, I too supported military forces capable of deterring enemies from threatening out security. "None but an armed nation can dispense with a standing army. To keep ours armed and disciplined is therefore at all times important, but especially so at a moment when rights the most essential to our welfare have been violated," and "For a people who are free and who mean to remain so, a well-organized and armed militia is their best security. It is, therefore, incumbent on us at every meeting [of Congress] to revise the condition of the militia and to ask ourselves if it is prepared to repel a powerful enemy at every point of our territories exposed to invasion... Congress alone has power to produce a uniform state of preparation in this great organ of defense. The interests which they so deeply feel in their own and their country's security will present this as among the most important objects of their deliberation."

MOD: It seems that you, Gentlemen, are all advocates for a balance of defense spending that would ensure a sufficient standing military force for self-defense but that at the same time prevents the military/industrial complex from excessively burdening the federal budget by unnecessary expenditures. I believe I will close on this subject of military spending with the comments, in 2011, of the senior military officer of the USA, the Chairman of the Joint Chiefs of Staff. When asked for his thoughts on the greatest threat to American national security, he replied "our debt."

Education:

MOD: Gentlemen, let's circle back to our discussion on the breadth of the powers of the federal government. The current American federal government has grown far beyond the enumerated powers that you gave it in 1787.

The tenth amendment to the US Constitution clearly states: "The powers not delegated to the United States by the Constitution, nor prohibited by it to the states, are reserved to the states respectively, or to the people."

The examples of the unconstitutional usurpation of undelegated powers by the federal government are too numerous to cite here, so I will pick a typical – and very expensive – example of this sad turn of events. Regulating education does not fall within the enumerated powers of the federal government. And yet, Congress established the US Department of Education, with five thousand federal employees and an annual budget of over $68,000,000,000 (billion) dollars in fiscal year 2014. Also, the American National Governors Association has recommended imposing a nationwide set of education standards called "Common Core."

Gentlemen, any thoughts?

TJ: That's outrageous! "If it is believed that... elementary schools will be better managed by the governor and council, the commissioners of the literary fund or any other general authority of the government than by the parents within each ward, it is a belief against all experience."

JM: My gosh yes! I second every word you said President Jefferson! If this state of affairs be true, how saddened I am to hear of such a grievous, unconstitutional taking of power by the federal government! Such actions were stridently opposed by me, Washington, and Jefferson. Recall President Washington's previous warning about the federal government taking for itself unconstitutional powers, no matter how good the pretext may be. Recall my previous comments on education:

"If Congress can apply money indefinitely to the general welfare... they may establish teachers in every State, county, and parish, and pay them out of the public Treasury; they may take into their own hands the education of children, establishing in like manner schools throughout the Union."

Is education an isolated example of the expansion of federal power?

MOD: No Sir, the federal government has its hands in everything from producing milk, to giving billions of taxpayer dollars a year to subsidize a new-fangled fuel called ethanol, to thousands upon thousands of environmental regulations that tell landowners when and what they can and cannot build on their property[8] - the list of federal powers is too extensive to accurately comprehend.

JM: What a disaster! Such a shame! I – all of us sitting here today - warned our posterity to not exceed the strictly enumerated, constitutional powers of the federal government! No wonder you all have more debt than your annual gross national product, increasing by billions of dollars every day!

And let me comment on the thousands of pages of federal regulations, to include your current federal tax code: "It will be of little avail to the people that the laws are made by men of their own choice, if the laws be so voluminous that they cannot be read, or so incoherent that they cannot be understood; if they be repealed or revised before they are put into effect, or undergo such incessant changes that no man who knows what the law is today can guess what it will be tomorrow. Law is defined to be a rule of action; but how can that be a rule, which is little known and less fixed?"

Is it true that the current Congress just passed a 2,000 page law regulating healthcare?

---

8   Do an Internet search on "Wyoming welder faces EPA fines." He faces $75,000/day in fines for building a pond on his eight acre, rural property. This EPA action represents the quintessential example of how citizens' liberty and property rights are taken by an out of control government agency, the creation of which is clearly beyond constitutionally enumerated federal government powers, funded to the tune of over $8 billion/yr.

MOD: Yes Sir, that is correct.

JM: Then what the Anti-Federalists feared so much has come true![9] The current size and scope of your federal government is far beyond its enumerated constitutional powers. By what you are telling me, Congress and the Executive branch have abused the "necessary and proper"and "general welfare" clauses.

"With respect to the words 'general welfare,' I have always regarded them as qualified by the detail of powers connected with them. To take them in a literal and unlimited sense would be a metamorphosis of the Constitution into a character which there is a host of proofs was not contemplated by its creators."

Below I provide the definitive answer to our discussion:

"The powers delegated by the...Constitution to the federal government are few and defined. Those which are to remain in the State governments are numerous and indefinite. The former [federal powers] will be exercised principally on external objects, [such] as war, peace, negotiation and foreign commerce...The powers reserved to the several States will extend to all the objects which in the ordinary course of affairs, concern the lives and liberties, and properties of the people, and the internal order, improvement and prosperity of the State."

"The accumulation of all powers, legislative, executive, and judiciary, in the same hands, whether of one, a few, or many, and whether hereditary, self-appointed, or elective, may justly be pronounced the very definition of tyranny."

---

9   The Anti-Federalists represented those who opposed the Constitution as it came out of the 1787 Constitutional Convention. The Federalists supported the Constitution and adamantly refuted the Anti-Federalist critic that the proposed Constitution would lead to a continually growing federal government that would meddle in every aspect of the citizenry's lives. The Federalists promised that Congress had no powers beyond those enumerated in the Constitution, and then went along with passing the Tenth Amendment to ensure restraint on federal government power. So much for promises – "if men were angels…"

TJ: I am in absolute agreement with President Madison. "If we can prevent the government from wasting the labors of the people, under the pretense of taking care of them, they must become happy."

MOD: Thank you Gentlemen for your comments – very sobering indeed.

End of this interview

Key quotes:

"The principle of spending money to be paid by posterity in the name of funding, is but swindling futurity on a large scale." Jefferson

"A wise and frugal government, which shall restrain men from injuring one another, shall leave them otherwise free to regulate their own pursuits of industry and improvement, and shall not take from the mouth of labor the bread it has earned. This is the sum of good government; and this is necessary to close the circle of our felicities." Jefferson

"If it is believed that... elementary schools will be better managed by the governor and council, the commissioners of the literary fund or any other general authority of the government than by the parents within each ward, it is a belief against all experience." Jefferson

"I think the best way of doing good to the poor, is not making them easy in poverty, but leading or driving them out of it. In my youth I travelled much, and I observed in different countries, that the more public provisions were made for the poor, the less they provided for themselves, and of course became poorer. And, on the contrary, the less was done for them, the more they did for themselves, and became richer." Franklin

"The government of the United States is a definite government, confined to specified objects. It is not like the state governments, whose powers are more general."

Moderator's Notes: *I could go on and on here about the intuitively obvious, unconstitutional growth of federal powers and the corresponding diminution of states' power.* The Affordable Care Act *of 2010 represents perhaps the most egregious expansion of federal power in modern history, adding thousands of pages of federal tax code that will increase the already excessively voluminous federal registers. And do we even need to rehash the Department of Education? Are we to believe that federal taxpayers need to pay $68,400,000,000 (billion, FY13 dollars) a year for education in America on top of what they already pay in local property and state income taxes? For that kind of cash, we ought to have the A-number 1 education system in the world – yet we certainly don't. Are we to believe, as Jefferson so pointedly states, that federal bureaucrats in Washington D.C. know how to better educate our kids than our local parents and school boards?* The Department of Education *is the classic example of federal bureaucrats meddling in the lives of the citizenry when they have no constitutional power to do so.* <u>*Is it any wonder that the total government debt exceeded the whole US gross domestic product (GDP) in the first two quarters of FY 2013 and still hovered around 100% of total GDP at the end of FY 2013?*</u>[10]

And let's not leave military spending out of this discussion. Excluding OCO (overseas contingency operations) funds used to fight the Iraq and Afghan wars, baseline spending, in constant 2001 dollars adjusted for inflation, increased nearly 40% from 2001 to 2013.[11] *Does the US need to spend almost 40% more on baseline defense, exclusive of OCO war funds, than it did in 2001 pre-9/11? How can that be? One main cause of this increase is politicians. They all want the Department of Defense (DoD) to be more cost effective, but politicians do not want a base or a unit, or a weapon system with jobs in their state/district, closed or cancelled, even when DoD recommends such actions. Civilian control of the military is a foundational constitutional principle, and Congress and the President have the authority to set military spending budget levels. But often times, these approvals are based on narrow, local political interests, rather than on what's good for the nation as a whole. The nation needs to spend money*

---

[10]   http://research.stlouisfed.org/fred2/series/GFDEGDQ188S

[11]   http://comptroller.defense.gov/Portals/45/Documents/defbudget/fy2014/ FY2014_Budget_Request_Overview_Book.pdf, (page 1-3)

to ensure a strong national defense, but not a dime more. The armed forces should not be used as a cash cow and jobs program for local and state governments, nor to artificially boost employment numbers.

Before we leave the subject of national defense, we must address the subject of war. Jefferson said, "In a long and bloody war, we lose many friends, and gain nothing." The US certainly needed to retaliate for the 9/11 attacks, but when it went on to conduct two "long and bloody" wars lasting close to/more than a decade, it appears that Jefferson was right – what have we gained and how many friends have we lost in Iraq and Afghanistan? No matter how good US motives might be, the road to hell (and war is hell) is often paved with good intentions.

But, there is no doubt that there are some within the military establishment who think more is always better when it comes to defense spending, especially if it is more for their slice of the pie. On numerous occasions, senior leaders advocate for programs not because they are a good use of public funds to defend the nation – but rather to perpetuate and/or increase their span of control and influence. This selfishness contributes to bloated defense budgets just as much as politicians bringing home the bacon by funneling government contracts to their districts and by prohibiting the closure of bases and weapon system production lines in their districts – even when the military says these bases and weapon systems are no longer needed.

Next, we come to the idea of the role of government in charity. It is hard to pin down an exact percentage of the federal budget that goes to entitlement programs, what I call charity: Social Security, Medicaid, unemployment benefits, Medicare, Food Stamps, housing assistance. So, let's be very conservative, and say that about 50% (probably much higher, but we'll go with 50%) of the budget goes to entitlement/charity programs. Total fiscal year 2013 federal government spending totaled about $3,500,000,000,000 (yes, that's right, "trillion") dollars. Fifty percent of that total equals $1,750,000,000,000 (trillion) that the government spends on charity programs.

Remember, the Father of the Constitution, James Madison, said, "The government of the United States is a definite government, confined to specified objects. It is not like the state governments, whose powers are more general. Charity is no part of the legislative duty of the government."

Thank you President Madison for making my next point before I did. I am not advocating for no government involvement in charity. I am forcefully pointing out that the obvious dichotomy of the Father of the Constitution saying the federal government has no role in public charity and the fact that over 50% of the federal budget is currently spent on charity – and that percentage is growing bigger every second of every hour of every day!

*We, the American people, have washed our hands of the Judeo-Christian call to look after our neighbors. We pay our federal and state taxes and wash our hands of the responsibility to look out for the poor, the tired, and the hungry. And the federal bureaucrats, always happy to increase their numbers and span of control, lick their chops every step of the way: "Send us more money! You can trust us! We will ensure that your money only goes to those who really need it. And, we promise that though you have sent us trillions of your dollars to create and run hundreds of federal departments, we will not use that money (and its power) to make thousands of pages or regulations that interfere in every area of your life." Right now, Americans, for the most part, send huge chunks of tax money to state and federal poverty programs, thinking "I sent in my taxes – I've done my part to help the poor – time to move on to other issues." Such an attitude leads to selfish hearts in the face of poverty. And, those huge chunks of cash flowing to the government increase its power and ability to squash individual liberty – **we are actually paying to lose our liberty!**

For those among us who are prosperous – here's a warning: one of the main causes of the French Revolution – where "the prosperous" had their prosperity forcibly removed by the revolutionaries – was the refusal of the prosperous to a) give up their special tax privileges (here would be included tax exemptions, loopholes, and subsidies for wealthy individuals and industries), and b) downright selfishness on the part of "the prosperous," aptly summarized by Marie Antoinette's supposed comments when told that the poor lacked bread, "let them eat cake!"

If "the prosperous" don't want the less fortunate coming after their prosperity (and this is occurring, because the less prosperous are more numerous and can vote politicians into office who will confiscate property for redistribution with more taxes at higher rates), they had better heed the Judeo-Christian value of charitable giving. Do you know that Americans, *on average, give about 1.5-2% of annual GDP to charity? How much should we give? The tithe would be a good place to start, 10%. How should we give it? Here's an example: the website Donorschoose.org allows teachers, often from schools in poor districts, to ask the general public for contributions to buy items such as reading material and multimedia equipment that the district cannot afford. Recently, I bought a $500 multimedia device for class in a local school near me. Within 25 miles of where I live, donorschoose.org shows about $12,500 of teacher requests. About 500,000 people live within 25 miles of where I live. Let's say about 250,000 of those people work or have a decent pension. To fund all of the teachers' requests, each person would need to give – wait for it - $20. Here's another idea for local charity. Go to your local department store and look for clearance clothes on sale. Buy some clearance clothes and give them to thrift stores or charities and churches that provide clothes to the needy. For $20, I bought 15 t-shirts on sale and gave them to a local thrift store whose proceeds are used to fund services for a safe house for battered women. These examples are how charity should – must! – be done in America – locally, on the ground, by citizens who want to help their fellow human beings. The best way to change America is not top down by the politicians. Rather, the change must come from the bottom up – one person, one household, one school, one community at a time. A solid house is not built from the top down, but from the bottom up, one brick at a time.*

Political hint – encourage charitable giving by providing better tax incentives, and charitable giving will go up – basic economics! There is plenty of wealth on the planet to go around. Those who have that wealth need to learn to loosen their grip on it, voluntarily, to give it to those who are needy – and worthy – of it. Herein lies a major reason why private charity is better than public charity – individuals are much better than a government bureaucracy at discerning the worthiness of those to whom charity is given.[12]

---

[12] In 2012 alone, the US Department of Agriculture estimated $750,000,000 (million), in food stamp fraud.
(*http://cnsnews.com/blog/joe-schoffstall/cost-food-stamp-fraud-more-doubles-three-years*)

Looking for some worthy charities to make the world a better place? How about helping the blind to see, the crippled to walk, and the deformed to be made whole! God could do these miracles by Himself, but I'm thinking He's waiting for all of us to do it for Him, to learn the lesson of "loving thy neighbor as thyself." He's already given us all the resources we need. Now, He's just waiting for us to break out of our selfishness to use them to love our neighbors more than ourselves.

- *So the blind can see - http://www.helpmesee.org/*
- *So the crippled can walk - http://cure.org/clubfoot*
- *So the deformed can be made whole - http://www.smiletrain.org/ or http://www.operationsmile.org/*
- *So the poor may be healed - http://www.mercyships.org/*

There are hundreds of other worthwhile charities doing good things for good people. The more resources they have, the more good they can do.[13]

Also, if you don't feel you are among "the prosperous," your time is just as, if not more, valuable than your money. A charity can have all the money in the world, but if people do not volunteer their time, charitable organizations are limited in the services they can provide. And even if you are among "the prosperous," you still ought to give some of your time to charitable deeds. Giving money is noble, but giving money and time is nobler still.

Many pundits that I read on this subject say that private charity could not make up for a significant decrease in governmental charitable spending. They use faulty logic by showing that even when taxes go down, charitable giving stays constant at about 2% of GDP. However, they fail to address this scenario: what if the government just cut, say, the Food Stamps program altogether? Are we to believe that Americans would leave their compatriots to starve to death in Boise, Albuquerque, New York City, Des Moines, Paducah, and all points in between? I say they would not! I say that Americans would rise to the occasion with their time – and their money – and that hunger would be reduced more in America by local folks focusing on local needs rather than an $80,000,000,000/yr (billion) Food Stamp program administered by Washington bureaucrats hundreds and

---

[13]   Charitynavigator.org & Givewell.org are good sites to check out charities.

thousands of miles away from those who need food. And, food aid would be distributed more efficiently and cost effectively.

Alexis De Tocqueville, a French aristocrat and politician, spent 9 months (May, 1831 to Feb, 1832) traveling around the US and studying our economic, social, and political systems. From his travels, he wrote what has become a classic in political science, Democracy in America. Tocqueville credited much of America's economic success and freedom to a spirit of self-sufficiency, without relying on government assistance. Indeed, he was astounded at the minimal presence and interference of the state and federal government in local affairs. He recounts how, for instance, if a tree were to fall and block a public road, the neighbors would most probably gather and take it upon themselves to clear the road.[14] Today, most neighborhoods would call down to city hall and say "hey, there's a tree blocking the road in front of my house. Someone needs to come and remove it" – a sad state of affairs as regards the mindset of modern American citizens and their increasing dependence on government to solve their problems and to make them more prosperous.

And speaking of prosperity, both Jefferson and Madison refute the concept of socialism and government redistribution of wealth among citizens. Both of these politically experienced and highly educated men realized that an "equal" partition of resources is an "unsolvable" impasse, and that in fact, it is the government's duty to protect, not redistribute, citizens' wealth and property that they have lawfully earned.

Now, in fairness, Jefferson did support distributing excess (after payment of government debts) federal revenue to the states for public works projects, to include education. But – and this is key - he believed that such a distribution should occur only in times of government surplus and that the distribution needed to be authorized by a constitutional amendment. Jefferson said, in relation to using federal money for these purposes, "as may be thought proper to add to the constitutional enumeration of federal powers" by "a corresponding amendment of the Constitution." Jefferson wanted this money to go to the states. He did not advocate for more federal bureaucracies. In fact, he continually tried to

---

[14]   *Democracy in America*, Part II, Chapter 4

suppress "unnecessary offices, of useless establishments and expenses" and internal taxes during his two presidential terms.

A few final thoughts on government and private property – we'll start with Lincoln:

"Property is the fruit of labor. Property is desirable - is a positive good in the world. That some should be rich, shows that others may become rich, and hence is just encouragement to industry and enterprise. Let not him who is houseless pull down the house of another; but let him labor diligently and build one for himself, thus by example assuring that his own shall be safe from violence when built."

Then Jefferson: "we must not let our rulers load us with perpetual debt. We must make our election between economy and liberty, or profusion and servitude. If we run into such debts, as that we must be taxed in our meat and in our drink, in our necessaries and our comforts, in our labors and our amusements…private fortunes are destroyed by public as well as by private extravagance."

And finally, going back to the Greeks, Aristotle taught that it is more important to equalize men's desires than their property – essentially to change peoples' heart to be more generous rather than to have government forcibly take their property. How do we do that? The next interview and the moderator's associated comments will answer this question.

CHAPTER 4

RELIGION IN AMERICA

"The Ten Commandments and the
Sermon on the Mount contain my Religion." John Adams

"Let us with caution indulge the supposition, that morality can
be maintained without religion. Whatever may be conceded to
the influence of refined education on minds of peculiar structure;
reason and experience both forbid us to expect that national
morality can prevail in exclusion of religious principle."

George Washington

MOD: Gentlemen – one of the great debates in American history centers on the role that religion played in the founding of the USA, and the role that religion should, or should not, have in political discourse. I have spent much time studying the religious commentary of our distinguished panel, as well as the writings of prominent historians on the subject, and I ask for your commentary on the following conclusion to which I have come: that the prevailing moral system of the founding principles of the USA is Judeo-Christian, and that you all intended that the country be founded upon Judeo-Christian values and principles, while still allowing freedom to worship any religion as a person's conscience dictates – or to not worship any deity at all.

Mr. Franklin, as the senior member of our panel today, I will offer you the first opportunity to comment on this topic.

BF: Well, this topic excited the passions of the populace in my day, and apparently this excitement has not abated over the centuries. Though I don't recall the term "Judeo-Christian" being in use during the 18th century, I can tell you that "the Faith you mention has doubtless its use in the world. I do not desire to see it diminished, nor would I endeavor to lessen it in any man. But I wish it were more productive of good works, than I have generally seen it: I mean real good works, works of kindness, charity, mercy, and public spirit; not holiday-keeping, sermon-reading or hearing; performing church ceremonies, or making long prayers, filled with flatteries and compliments, despised even by wise men, and much less capable of pleasing the Deity. The worship of God is a duty; the hearing and reading of sermons may be useful; but, if men rest in hearing and praying, as too many do, it is as if a tree should value itself on being watered and putting forth leaves, though it never produced any fruit."

And, I am pleased to see that President Lincoln recalled in his speeches my sentiments when I said during the Constitutional Convention: "We have been assured, Sir, in the Sacred Writings, that except the Lord build the House, they labor in vain who build it. I've lived, Sir, a long time, and the longer I live, the more convincing proofs I see of this truth — that God governs in the affairs of men."

MOD: Do you consider yourself to be a Christian, in the sense of believing in Jesus Christ's divinity and that his death on the cross atones for all of mankind's sins?

BF: "As to Jesus of Nazareth, my opinion of whom you particularly desire, I think the system of morals and his religion, as He left them to us, the best the world ever saw or is likely to see; but I apprehend it has received various corrupt changes, and I have, with most of the present dissenters in England, some doubts as to His divinity; though it is a question I do not dogmatize upon."

TJ: If I may, I too would like to respond to the question about being Christian, as much has been written about my religious beliefs, yet few refer to my own words. So, I wish to clarify my position: "To the corruptions of Christianity I am indeed opposed; but not to the genuine precepts of Jesus himself. I am a Christian, in the only sense he wished any one to be; sincerely attached to his doctrines, in preference to all others; ascribing to himself every human excellence, & believing he never claimed any other."

MOD: President Jefferson, is it true that you made a book called *The Philosophy of Jesus*?

TJ: Yes, that is true. "It is a paradigma[15] of his doctrines, made by cutting the texts out of the book [the Bible] and arranging them on the pages of a blank book, in a certain order of time or subject. A more beautiful or precious morsel of ethics I have never seen."

JA: And I too concur with Mr. Franklin and President Jefferson. "The Christian religion is, above all the religions that ever prevailed or existed in ancient or modern times, the religion of wisdom, virtue, equity and humanity."

GW: I will add to the above commentary. During my tenure as Commander of the US Army during the Revolution, I desired that "every man will endeavor to live and act as becomes a Christian soldier defending the dearest rights and liberties of this country."

Furthermore, I wrote to Brigadier General Thomas Nelson in 1778, during the Revolutionary war, that "The Hand of Providence has been so conspicuous in all this, that he must be worse than an infidel that lacks faith, and more than wicked, that has not gratitude enough to acknowledge his obligations."

MOD: Gentlemen, it seems that you are all pretty much in agreement that the Judeo-Christian moral system forms the basis of your personal

---

[15]   "Paradigma" is an obsolete spelling of "paradigm," a system or framework of assumptions.

ethical codes, though you have variances in your beliefs about the core precepts of Christianity. Let us move on to the issues of religion in the founding of the country and of religion in political life. I start our discussion with this provocative historical fact: the Treaty of Tripoli, signed by the USA and Tripolitania[16] in 1797, clearly states, "As the Government of the United States of America is not, in any sense, founded on the Christian religion...it has in itself no character of enmity against the laws, religion, or tranquility, of Mussulmen [Muslims]."

Additionally, President Adams, you once wrote "Although the detail of the formation of the American governments is at present little known or regarded either in Europe or America, it may hereafter become an object of curiosity. It will never be pretended that any persons employed in that service had any interviews with the gods, or were in any degree under the inspiration of heaven, any more than those at work upon ships or houses, or laboring in merchandize or agriculture: it will forever be acknowledged that these governments were contrived merely by the use of reason and the senses."

One could surmise that you all believed that religion plays no part in American government. Would you gentlemen say that is true?

"Let us with caution indulge the supposition, that morality can be maintained without religion. Whatever may be conceded to the influence of refined education on minds of peculiar structure; reason and experience both forbid us to expect that national morality can prevail in exclusion of religious principle [emphasis added]."

In a letter I wrote in June, 1783, I earnestly prayed "that God would... incline the hearts of the citizens to cultivate a spirit of subordination & obedience to government, to entertain a brotherly affection and love for one another, for their fellow citizens of the United States at large and particularly for their brethren who have served in the field—and finally that he would most graciously be pleased to dispose us all to do justice, to love mercy and to demean ourselves, with that charity, humility and pacific temper of mind, which were the characteristics of the Divine Author of our blessed religion and *without an humble*

---

[16] Tripolitania was an area of the Ottoman Empire along what is today the coast of Libya.

imitation of whose example in these things, we can never hope to be a happy Nation [emphasis added]."

JM: If I may, "The belief in a God all powerful wise and good, is so essential to the moral order of the world and to the happiness of man, that arguments which enforce it cannot be drawn from too many sources nor adapted with too much solicitude [care] to the different characters and capacities to be impressed with it."

JA: I wholeheartedly agree with President Washington, for "our Constitution was made only for a moral and religious people. It is wholly inadequate to the government of any other."

However, "government has no right to hurt the hair of an atheist for his opinions."

MOD: Another good segue, President Adams. Gentlemen, there seems to be no doubt that you are all God fearing men with a belief in a Judeo-Christian deity, and that Judeo-Christian values permeate your characters as well as the founding principles of America. But what about those people who do not follow a Judeo-Christian faith – are they welcome in the USA?

TJ: In 1779, many years before the ratification of the American Constitution, the Virginia State Legislature passed a law to guarantee religious freedom. "Where the preamble [to the law] declares that coercion is a departure from the plan of the holy author of our religion, an amendment was proposed, by inserting the word 'Jesus Christ,' so that it should read, 'a departure from the plan of Jesus Christ, the holy author of our religion.' The insertion was rejected by a great majority, in proof that they meant to comprehend, within the mantle of its protection, the Jew and the Gentile, the Christian and Muslim, the Hindu, and infidel of every denomination."

MOD: Well – it seems that you, President Jefferson, believe that freedom of religion is an essential feature of our national morality and political prosperity. But let's get more specific in regards to the question of religion in government discourse. President Jefferson, you are often held up as the icon of the "separation of church and state" because of the letter you wrote to the Danbury Baptists where you said, "I contemplate with sovereign reverence that act of the whole American people which declared that their legislature should 'make no law respecting an establishment of religion, or prohibiting the free exercise thereof,' thus building a wall of separation between Church & State."

And in a letter to the Presbyterian Minister Samuel Miller, you stated, "I do not believe it is for the interest of religion to invite the civil magistrate to direct its exercises, its discipline, or its doctrines; nor of the religious societies that the general government should be invested with the power of effecting any uniformity of time or matter among them....I am aware that the practice of my predecessors may be quoted....Be this as it may, everyone must act according to the dictates of his own reason, and mine tells me that civil powers alone have been given to the President of the U.S. and no authority to direct the religious exercises of his constituents."

But, President Jefferson, you also signed laws that provided for Christian missionaries and Bibles for American Indians, and you make reference in your first inaugural address to "acknowledging and affirming an overruling providence," and in your second inaugural address, you seem to ask for God's blessing upon your presidency and the nation as a whole, stating, "I shall need, too, the favor of that Being in whose hands we are, who led our forefathers, as Israel of old, from their native land, and planted them in a country flowing with all the necessaries and comforts of life; who has covered our infancy with his providence, and our riper years with his wisdom and power; and to whose goodness I ask you to join with me in supplications, that he will so enlighten the minds of your servants, guide their councils, and prosper their measures, that whatsoever they do, shall result in your good, and shall secure to you the peace, friendship, and approbation of all nations."

President Jefferson, with respect, I would like to point out that your words about a strict separation between government and religion do not necessarily square with some of your actions as President as well as your inaugural proclamations as President.

Is your position that religion has no place whatsoever in politics and that it should be excluded completely from the government?

TJ: I did indeed make the statements you cite and took the actions you mentioned. I led a long life in public service. I wrote thousands of pages of documents, and I made innumerable decisions during my tenure as a public servant. I will let those words and actions speak for themselves to posterity as to my views on religion and government, and I yield the floor on this issue to the other members of this distinguished panel.

MOD: Secretary Hamilton, is it true that you tried to create an organization named The Christian Constitutional Society in 1802?

AH: Yes, that is true. The purpose of the organization was to be -

1st   The support of the Christian Religion.
2nd   The support of the Constitution of the United States.

I believed that such a society was necessary at the time to bring Christian values into political discourse to help resolve political problems in the USA.[17]

MOD: Mr. Franklin, did you propose that the Constitutional Convention open its sessions with a prayer to ask for Divine assistance in overcoming some of the implacable obstacles that the Convention was facing?

BF: Yes, I did, and the motion was seconded, but "the convention, except three or four persons, thought prayer unnecessary." However, I will point out that upon the convocation of the first Constitutional Congress, two chaplains were hired, one for the House, and one for the Senate, to provide prayers for Congressional sessions, and it appears that this practice has been continued to the present day.

---

[17]   In this passage, I have summarized Hamilton's explanation on the need for The Christian Constitutional Society. Hamilton proposed this society in a letter to James Bayard in Apr, 1802.

GW: If I may, please, I would like to make the following point. It is true that the first amendment to the Constitution proscribes the establishment of a national religion by the government. However, I do want to recall my exhortation that I made at the end of my first inaugural speech to my fellow Americans in regards to government and God:

"I shall take my present leave; but not without resorting once more to the benign Parent of the human race, in humble supplication that since he has been pleased to favor the American people, with opportunities for deliberating in perfect tranquility, and dispositions for deciding with unparalleled unanimity on a form of government, for the security of their Union, and the advancement of their happiness; so this divine blessing may be equally conspicuous in the enlarged views—the temperate consultations, and the wise measures on which the success of this government must depend."

MOD: President Madison, have you anything to say on these issues?

JM: I believe my views to be closely aligned with President Jefferson. I did make several Presidential Prayer Proclamations during my presidency, but I did write what has come to be known as "The Detached Memorandum" in which I disapproved of using public money to hire congressional and military chaplains, and I generally disapproved of public proclamations of prayer by government officials.

MOD: President Lincoln, with the reflection of four score and seven years of American history under your belt during your presidency, what role do you believe religion plays in governmental affairs?

AL: I recommend to you simply the words I spoke during my first inaugural address on the eve of the Civil War: "Intelligence, patriotism, Christianity, and a firm reliance on Him who has never yet forsaken this favored land are still competent to adjust in the best way all our present difficulty."

End of this interview

Key quotes:

"Of all the dispositions and habits which lead to political prosperity, Religion and Morality are indispensable supports. In vain would that man claim the tribute of Patriotism, who should labor to subvert these great pillars of human happiness, these firmest props of the duties of men and citizens. The mere politician, equally with the pious man, ought to respect and to cherish them. A volume could not trace all their connections with private and public felicity." Washington

"Let us with caution indulge the supposition, that morality can be maintained without religion. Whatever may be conceded to the influence of refined education on minds of peculiar structure; reason and experience both forbid us to expect that national morality can prevail in exclusion of religious principle." Washington

Moderator's Notes: Before we leave the topic of religion in America, as a practicing Christian, I feel obliged to make a few comments. I have spent hundreds of hours reading hundreds of documents from the Founding Fathers on their personal religious views and on their views of government, politics, and religion. I have come to the following conclusions. First, the Founding Fathers represented a range of religious fervor - Washington and Adams being on the more religious side, Franklin and Hamilton somewhere in between, with Madison and Jefferson showing less religious fervor. Second, all the Founding Fathers here mentioned believed in a Divinity that should be worshipped, and that Divinity is the Judeo-Christian God of the Bible, leading to my last conclusion that Judeo-Christian morals and ethics formed the basis of the personal morality of the Founding Fathers, and the basis on which the elements of American government were formed.

Before I seriously started doing the research for these interviews, I intuitively knew that the Judeo-Christian ethic formed the basis of the American political and cultural system. I asked myself how that ethic could be boiled down into something that most Americans, religious or not, could agree upon. I thought I had hit upon a grand idea of using the Ten Commandments (Old Testament, Judeo) and the Sermon on the Mount (New Testament, Christian) as the foundation of the Judeo-Christian ethic. When I saw that John Adams had come to this conclusion centuries before I did, I was at first disappointed, because my pride wanted that idea to be "mine." But, my better sense took hold, and I realized that Adam's words proved what I was intuitively trying to solidify. And, when I saw that Jefferson actually said he believed in the moral philosophy of Jesus Christ "in preference to all others," I knew instantly that my intuition had been true.*

*Note: If you read the Ten Commandments and the Sermon on the Mount, you will notice that there is no mention of gay marriage; private, not public charity, is encouraged; stealing and coveting are prohibited (like envying what others have and then voting for politicians to pass laws to "redistribute" other folk's money); all folks get the same divine advice and are held to the same moral standards regardless of their race, country of origin, or skin color; excessive court litigation is highly discouraged; adultery is prohibited and divorce is discouraged; turning the other cheek is encouraged as opposed to revenge; praying is encouraged; worrying about the future is discouraged; judging others is discouraged unless you've got all the problems in your own life worked out; and the meek get to inherit the earth – doesn't sound much like America today in 2014.

PROPOSAL FOR CULTURE WAR TRUCE! I propose a truce in the culture wars. The political Right needs to give up its fight against gay marriage and grant full civil rights to gay people. The Right also needs to pick its battles in the abortion area: prohibit abortion except in cases of incest, rape, and when the life of the mother is in danger; and prohibit late term abortions when a baby is viable outside of the womb (unless the mother's life is in danger). The Left needs to give up its property redistribution (legalized theft) legislative agenda, as well as its divisive agenda of governmental goodies and privileges for a certain gender and for certain races. It is "self-evident" that all persons are "created equal." This equality is before the law. It is certainly not an equality of property or even an equality of opportunity (trying to get the same opportunities in life for 300 million Americans may sound pleasing to the mind, but it is realistically impossible to achieve). The 20th century Russian and

Chinese Revolutions, among other utopian experiments (the Killing Fields of Cambodia come to mind), have horrifyingly shown the foolhardiness of these utopian schemes.

> *"Equally fallacious [misleading] is the doctrine of 'equality,' of which much is said, and little understood. That one man in a state, has as good a right as another to his life, limbs, reputation and property, is a proposition that no man will dispute. Nor will it be denied that each member of a society, who has not forfeited his claims by misconduct, has an equal right to protection. But if by 'equality,' writers understand an equal right to distinction, and influence; or if they understand an equal share of talents and bodily powers; in these senses, all men are not equal." Noah Webster, 1802*

The American government needs to stop picking "favorite Americans" and to start applying the laws equally to all Americans, with no regard for skin color, racial origin, sex, or sexual orientation (although I do not mean that businesses must hire men who choose to come to work dressed as women, or that female public bathrooms and locker rooms, especially in schools, must be open to boys if they feel like girls. There are common sense limits to transforming every personal peculiarity into a "civil right").

A famous man had a dream that people in America should be judged by their character, not by the color of their skin. As long as the government plays favorites via affirmative action programs and "goals" (really quotas) for certain classes of citizens to receive government contracts, among a myriad of other special privileges given to some citizens and not to others, that famous man's dream will never come true – but it should come true – it must come true – for America to be all that it can be.

Additionally, no discussion of religion and the Founders would be complete without addressing "Deism," the idea that a Deity created the world, and then set it in motion like a clock, without any further intervention. Many historians and authors have tried to paint the Founders as this kind of Deist, but even a cursory reading of their comments on religion reveals that the Founders believed in a Deity whose hand played a role, indeed a defining role, in the affairs of mankind. The quotations in this chapter strongly refute those who support the idea that the Founders were Deists.

Finally, some comments on the French Revolution and religion (and the lack thereof), because the French Revolution followed closely on the heels of the American Revolution. The American Declaration of Independence was written in 1776. Thirteen years later, 1789, France, probably the most civilized country on the European continent at the time, solidified its own revolution, with its Declaration of the Rights of Man, which seems closely aligned with the concepts in the Declaration of Independence primarily authored by Jefferson – who just happened to be in Paris in 1789 as the American Minister to France. However, the French Revolution quickly took on a nasty, anti-religious tone: churches were looted, destroyed, or turned into warehouses and granaries, among other uses. The French Revolutionary Government instituted the Civil Constitution of the Clergy that required all clergy members to take a vow of loyalty to the French Constitution and brought all church property under state control. As the French Revolution progressed, it became more and more anti-religious, and above and beyond the many thousands who lost their heads to the guillotine's blade in Paris, tens of thousands of French men, women, and children were slaughtered throughout France in the name of "liberty, equality, fraternity." As one of the main leaders of the French Revolution, Maximilien de Robespierre supposedly said, "you have to break a few eggs to make an omelet." Robespierre eventually fell out of favor with the increasingly radical revolutionary leaders; ironically and predictably, his head became part of the omelet.

My point? During the American Revolution and during the Constitutional Convention, the Judeo-Christian ethic was ever present, and there were no widespread efforts by the American populace or American political leaders to remove religion from the public arena. Ergo, political opponents did not chop off each other's heads by the thousands, and armed bands of thugs were not sent out by those in favor of the Constitution to round up and kill by the thousands those who might be opposed to the Constitution, and vice versa. The American Revolution, based on Judeo-Christian values and supplications by the revolutionaries to a beneficent God to guide their actions and to protect their country, resulted in a Constitution that has stood the test of time for the last 225 years, and has produced the most prosperous and powerful country in the history of mankind. The French Revolution, as it became more and more anti-religious, also became more and more violent and murderous, leading eventually to Napoleon's dictatorship and more than 20 years of constant war against its European neighbors. In fact, most of the godless revolutions since the French Revolution, such as the Russian Revolution and the Chinese Revolution*, have resulted in the murder and starvation of tens of millions of people, and a denial of even the most basic of human rights, in order that mankind be, as Rousseau infamously and oxymoronically said a few years prior to the French Revolution, "forced to be free."**

*I am not asserting that Americans are better people because the American Revolution was less violent that the French, Chinese, or Russian Revolutions; human nature is human nature, no matter the country. I am asserting that by staying true to a tried and tested religious moral standard, the Founders, and the American populace at large, avoided the violent excesses and human rights abuses that eventually befell the French, Russian, and Chinese Revolutions. As Lord Acton said, "Political atheism: Ends justifies the means. This is still the most widespread of all the opinions inimical to liberty," and "Power tends to corrupt, and absolute power corrupts absolutely." When human beings chuck the idea of an eternal moral standard above the human mind, then the human mind becomes its own god, and human "reason" becomes the standard by which actions are judged. I'm sure those who had Robespierre's head lopped off, as well as Lenin, Mao, Guevara, and all the other anti-religious revolutionaries, all had good "reasons" for executing, starving, torturing, and brutalizing their fellow countrymen by the tens of millions.

**These comments on France are presented for historical comparison purposes and not as a rebuke of the French nation. In fact, the Franks (later to become the French) under Charles the Hammer, at the battle of Poitiers (near present day Tours, France), in 732, stopped the conquering of Western Europe by invading Arab armies: it's not too far of a stretch to say that the victory at Poitiers saved Western European civilization. Franks and the French have played a major role on the world stage since 1066. In that year, William the Conqueror (from what was at the time the Duchy of Normandy, a fiefdom in present day northern France) invaded England. As the French nobility poured into England, the English and French languages became inextricably and permanently linked (a good

30% or so of modern English words have some sort of French origin). At the battle of Yorktown in 1781, the French saved the burgeoning American republic, and the Americans, 163 years later on the beaches of Normandy, were the driving force in saving the French from Nazism. One need only look at the American names of streets in Paris, and the French names of towns across America (Lafayette, Des Moines, Coeur d'Alene), to see that our lives, our cultures, and our fortunes have been, for over two centuries, and continue to be, mutually linked. Vive l'amitié Franco-Américaine (long live Franco-American friendship)!

One last point on religion in America – everyone seems to know about the supposed "separation of church and state" in the American Constitution? Not so fast! First, let's recall the First Amendment to the American Constitution.

"Congress shall make no law respecting an establishment of religion, or prohibiting the free exercise thereof; or abridging the freedom of speech, or of the press; or the right of the people peaceably to assemble, and to petition the Government for a redress of grievances."

Here's the truth about this amendment; it was supposed to do two things: prohibit the federal government (but not the state governments) from establishing a national, government sponsored religion; and - this is what we all seem to forget - to prohibit the federal government from interfering in citizens' free exercise thereof. So, where did all this "can't pray in school, can't pray before a football game, can't pray at a high school graduation" prohibition come from? Well, the answer is debatable, but in the decision of the Supreme Court case Everson v. Board of Education in 1947, the majority stated "In the words of Jefferson, the clause against establishment of religion by law was intended to erect 'a wall of separation between Church and State.'" It is disturbing that the Supreme Court used a letter from Thomas Jefferson, and not the plain language of the Constitution itself, to ban religion from public school Christmas concerts, as well as from national parks and cemeteries. Go back and read Washington's quotes – all the quotes above – about religion, morality, and the public good. The Founders never meant to ban religion from public institutions – in fact, they said religion was essential to the good moral order and prosperity of a country and its political order. The Founders merely meant to keep the federal government from establishing a national religion – and nothing more – a fact evidenced by the words "or prohibiting the free exercise thereof" stated right after the national religion ban.

"As the union between spiritual freedom and political liberty seems nearly inseparable, it is our duty to defend both. " Thomas Paine

"As the safety and prosperity of nations ultimately and essentially depend on the protection and blessing of Almighty God; and the national acknowledgment of this truth is not only an indispensable duty, which the people owe to him, but a duty whose natural influence is favorable to the promotion of that morality and piety, without which social happiness cannot exist, nor the blessings of a free government be enjoyed; and as this duty, at all times incumbent, is so especially in seasons of difficulty and of danger, when existing or threatening calamities, the just judgments of God against prevalent iniquity, are a loud call to repentance and reformation; and as the United States of America are at present placed in a hazardous and afflictive situation…it has appeared to me that the duty of imploring the mercy and benediction of Heaven on our country, demands at this time a special attention from its inhabitants." President John Adams, 1798.

A final thought on gay marriage – I am not in favor of gay marriage. I believe that marriage is a sacred union of the soul of one man and one woman. But in our society, marriage provides people with legal rights: inheritance, end of life decisions, tax benefits, etc. In keeping with the idea that all Americans should be equal before the law, I propose that "civil union" replace the word "marriage" in all of our laws and civil documents. As it is in France, let the government provide a legal union between two people (and only two people of legal age), and let religious establishments perform marriages. Proponents and opponents of gay marriage will never agree on the issue. However, my proposal provides a compromise that keeps marriage as sacred and holy while simultaneously ensuring that all Americans receive equal legal protection and rights under US law in accordance with the 14th Amendment to the US Constitution.

Let us move on…

CHAPTER 5

AMERICAN PATRIOTISM – WHAT DOES IT MEAN TO BE "AN AMERICAN?"

"I am not a Virginian, but an American." Patrick Henry

MOD: Gentlemen, I'm sure you all a consider yourselves to be Americans, and you are proud of that appellation. Yet, the question seems to hang in the air: what does it mean to be American?

The 26th American President, Theodore Roosevelt, stated:

> "In the first place we should insist that if the immigrant who comes here in good faith becomes an American and assimilates himself to us, he shall be treated on an exact equality with everyone else, for it is an outrage to discriminate against any such man because of creed, or birthplace, or origin. But this is predicated upon the man's becoming in very fact an American, and nothing but an American. If he tries to keep segregated with

men of his own origin and separated from the rest of America, then he isn't doing his part as an American. There can be no divided allegiance here. Any man who says he is an American, but something else also, isn't an American at all. We have room for but one flag, the American flag, and this excludes the red flag, which symbolizes all wars against liberty and civilization, just as much as it excludes any foreign flag of a nation to which we are hostile. We have room for but one language here, and that is the English language, for we intend to see that the crucible turns our people out as Americans, of American nationality, and not as dwellers in a polyglot boarding-house; and we have room for but one soul loyalty, and that is loyalty to the American people."

In modern America, people now call themselves "XXXX-American," with Hispanic, African, and Asian being among the most popular, but certainly not the only, monikers added before "American."[18] But in Roosevelt's opinion, an American should be "nothing but an American… Any man who says he is an American, but something else also, isn't an American at all."

And the American citizenship oath clearly requires that American citizens "renounce and abjure all allegiance and fidelity to any foreign prince, potentate, state, or sovereignty, of whom or which I have heretofore been a subject or citizen."

American citizens are supposed to be "just American."

---

[18] And, even though there are more females than males in America, the US Department of Labor has a "Women's Bureau" and an "Office of Small and Disadvantaged Business Utilization," which has, as one of its expressed purposes, "to ensure procurement opportunities for women-owned businesses." I thought the Civil Rights Act prohibited discrimination based on gender? Oh, that's right, the Supreme Court (the supposed guarantor of equality of all citizens before the law) declared that discrimination is permissible, but only for the government, as long as there is a "compelling government interest" - according to government bureaucrats.

Does anyone have any comments to make on this topic?

GW: Yes, most certainly. I welcomed all people to be Americans. But I told my countrymen that "citizens by birth or choice, of a common country, that country [USA] has a right to concentrate your affections. The name of American, which belongs to you, in your national capacity, must always exalt the just pride of patriotism, more than any appellation derived from local discriminations. With slight shades of difference, you have the same religion, manners, habits, and political principles. You have in a common cause fought and triumphed together; the independence and liberty you possess are the work of joint councils, and joint efforts, of common dangers, sufferings and successes."

"The bosom of America is open to receive not only the opulent & respectable stranger, but the oppressed & persecuted of all nations & religions; whom we shall welcome to a participation of all our rights & privileges, if by decency & propriety of conduct they appear to merit the enjoyment."

"I had always hoped that this land might become a safe & agreeable asylum to the virtuous & persecuted part of mankind, to whatever nation they might belong," with the expectation that "every reflecting and virtuous mind…exhibit the continuance of the Union as a primary object of patriotic desire."

MOD: President Washington, I believe you will be happy to know that your sentiments on immigration are now echoed in a beautiful poem engraved on a large Statue of Liberty, given to the USA in 1875 by our ally France:

"The New Colossus"
Not like the brazen giant of Greek fame,
With conquering limbs astride from land to land;
Here at our sea-washed, sunset gates shall stand
A mighty woman with a torch, whose flame
Is the imprisoned lightning, and her name Mother of Exiles.
From her beacon-hand
Glows world-wide welcome; her mild eyes command

The air-bridged harbor that twin cities frame.
"Keep ancient lands, your storied pomp!" cries she with silent lips.
"Give me your tired, your poor, Your huddled masses yearning to breathe free,
The wretched refuse of your teeming shore.
Send these, the homeless, tempest-tost to me,
I lift my lamp beside the golden door!"

Emma Lazarus

GW: Outstanding! May the fertile shores and open plains of the USA always be a harbor of peace and prosperity for the oppressed peoples of the world.

JM: Yes Sir, President Washington, I agree that there are advantages to immigration, but "when we are considering the advantages that may result from an easy mode of naturalization, we ought also to consider the cautions necessary to guard against abuses; it is no doubt very desirable, that we should hold out as many inducements as possible, for the worthy part of mankind to come and settle amongst us, and throw their fortunes into a common lot with ours. But, why is this desirable? Not merely to swell the catalogue of people. No, sir, 'tis to increase the wealth and strength of the community, and those who acquire the rights of citizenship, without adding to the strength or wealth of the community, are not the people we are in want of…I should be exceeding sorry, sir, that our rule of naturalization excluded a single person of good fame, that really meant to incorporate himself into our society; on the other hand, I do not wish that any man should acquire the privilege, but who, in fact, is a real addition to the wealth or strength of the United States."

MOD: Thank you gentlemen, for your comments. Apparently, part of the original intent of being American meant open arms to all peoples of the world, tempered by caution against opening American borders to those people who might be injurious to our nation and to those who would not incorporate themselves into American society. But coming back around to the idea of being American, does anyone have further comments to make?

TJ: Yes, I do. "Let us reflect that having banished from our land that religious intolerance under which mankind so long bled and suffered, we have yet gained little if we countenance a political intolerance."

"We have called by different names brethren of the same principle. We are all republicans: we are all federalists. If there be any among us who would wish to dissolve this Union, or to change its republican form, let them stand undisturbed as monuments of the safety with which error of opinion may be tolerated, where reason is left free to combat it."

"Let us then, with courage and confidence, pursue our own federal and republican principles; our attachment to union and representative government... entertaining a due sense of our equal right to the use of our own faculties, to the acquisitions of our own industry, to honor and confidence from our fellow citizens, resulting not from birth, but from our actions and their sense of them, enlightened by a benign religion, professed indeed and practiced in various forms, yet all of them inculcating honesty, truth, temperance, gratitude and the love of man, acknowledging and adoring an overruling providence, which by all its dispensations proves that it delights in the happiness of man here, and his greater happiness hereafter."

Let us ensure "Equal and exact justice to all men, of whatever state or persuasion, religious or political:—peace, commerce, and honest friendship with all nations, entangling alliances with none; the support of the state governments in all their rights, as the most competent administrations for our domestic concerns, and the surest bulwarks against anti-republican tendencies; the preservation of the general government in its whole constitutional vigor, as the sheet anchor of our peace at home, and safety abroad: a jealous care of the right of election by the people...absolute acquiescence in the decisions of the majority, the vital principle of republics...a well-disciplined militia, our best reliance in peace, and for the first moments of war, till regulars may relieve them; the supremacy of the civil over the military authority; economy in the public expense, that labor may be lightly burdened; the honest payment of our debts and sacred preservation of the public faith; encouragement of agriculture, and of commerce as its handmaid; the diffusion of information, and arraignment of all abuses at the bar of the public reason; freedom of religion; freedom of the press; and freedom of person, under the protection of the Habeas Corpus; and trial by juries impartially selected. These principles form the bright constellation, which has gone before us and guided our steps through an age of revolution and reformation. The wisdom of our sages, and blood of our heroes have been devoted to their attainment: they should be the creed of our political faith; the text of civic instruction, the touchstone by which to try the services of those we trust; and should we wander from them in moments of error or of alarm, let us hasten to retrace our steps, and to regain the road which alone leads to peace, liberty and safety."

JM: With President Jefferson's wise comments, I must concur and add that Americans must "hold the Union of the States as the basis of their peace and happiness; to support the Constitution, which is the cement of the Union, as well in its limitations as in its authorities; to respect the rights and authorities reserved to the States and to the people, as equally incorporated with, and essential to the success of, the general system; to avoid the slightest interference with the rights of conscience, or the functions of religion so wisely exempted from civil jurisdiction; to preserve in their full energy, the other salutary provisions in behalf of private and personal rights, and of the freedom of the press; to observe economy in public expenditures; to liberate the public resources by an honorable discharge of the public debts...to promote by authorized means, improvements friendly to agriculture, to manufactures and to external as well as internal commerce; to favor, in like manner, the advancement of science and the diffusion of information as the best aliment to true liberty."

BF: Sirs, if I may, I would like to remind us of the highlights of a letter I wrote in 1784 while living in Paris. The letter's subject concerned that type of person that would be well suited to immigrate to America. The letter was lengthy, so I will summarize:

- In America, people, of a stranger, do not inquire concerning a stranger, "What is he?" but "What can he do?" If he has any useful art, he is welcome; and if he exercises it, and behaves well, he will be respected by all that know him.

- The people have a saying, that God Almighty is himself a mechanic, the greatest in the universe; and he is respected and admired more for the variety, ingenuity, and utility of his handyworks, than for the antiquity of his family.

- With regard to encouragements for strangers from government, they are really only what are derived from good laws and liberty. Strangers are welcome, because there is room enough for them all, and therefore the old inhabitants are not jealous of them; the laws protect them sufficiently, so that they have no need of the patronage of great men; and every one will enjoy securely the profits of his industry. But, if he does not bring a fortune with him, he must work and be industrious to live. But the government does not at present, whatever it may have done in former times, hire people to become settlers, by paying...any other kind of emolument [compensation] whatsoever.

- Tolerably good workmen...are sure to find employ, and to be well paid for their work, there being no restraints preventing strangers from exercising any art they understand, nor any permission necessary. If they are poor, they begin first as servants or journeymen; and if they are sober, industrious, and frugal, they soon become masters, establish themselves in business, marry, raise families, and become respectable citizens.

- Those, who desire to understand the state of government in America, would do well to read the Constitutions of the several states, and the Articles of Confederation that bind the whole together for general purposes, under the Direction of one Assembly, called the Congress. These Constitutions have been printed, by order of Congress, in America; two editions of them have also been printed in London; and a good translation of them into French has lately been published at Paris.

- The almost general mediocrity of fortune that prevails in America obliging its people to follow some business for subsistence, those vices, that arise usually from idleness, are in a great measure prevented. Industry and constant employment are great preservatives of the morals and virtue of a nation. Hence bad examples to youth are more rare in America, which must be a comfortable consideration to parents.

- Serious religion, under its various denominations, is not only tolerated, but respected and practiced... And the Divine Being seems to have manifested his approbation of the mutual forbearance and kindness with which the different sects treat each other, by the remarkable prosperity with which He has been pleased to favor the whole country.

MOD: Sirs, I must profess my admiration and gratefulness for all of your efforts to make the United States a beacon of freedom, hope, and prosperity for the people of every race, creed, skin color, and language. Let us all hope that the beacon has not grown too dim and that we, your progeny, will have the wisdom to make it shine ever and ever brighter.

End of this interview

Key quotes:

"Citizens by birth or choice, of a common country, that country [USA] has a right to concentrate your affections. The name of American, which belongs to you, in your national capacity, must always exalt the just pride of patriotism, more than any appellation derived from local discriminations." Washington

"I had always hoped that this land might become a safe & agreeable asylum to the virtuous & persecuted part of mankind, to whatever nation they might belong." Washington

"But, why is this [immigration] desirable? Not merely to swell the catalogue of people. No, sir, 'tis to increase the wealth and strength of the community, and those who acquire the rights of citizenship, without adding to the strength or wealth of the community, are not the people we are in want of." Madison

Moderator's Notes: *American exceptionalism exists and can be defined with some certainty. Being American means adhering to a Judeo-Christian system of morals and values (which can be done without being Judeo-Christian and still having freedom of religion) and accepting Washington's and Adam's admonition that the US Constitution and Republic can only be preserved by constant reference to the Bible and Judeo-Christian virtues. Being American means believing in the permanent union of the states in a federal republic, where the government does not treat citizens differently based on their skin color, national origin, or gender. Additionally, the original Americans believed in keeping the federal government limited in power and scope by allowing it to exercise only those powers specifically granted to it in the Constitution and by narrowly interpreting those powers to avoid excessive governmental growth, which inevitably leads to increasing rates of taxation and control for an ever expanding government. Furthermore, frugality in government expenditure and avoiding excessive public debt rank high on the American value list. Finally, Americans believe in governance at the local level and free markets where, as Jefferson points out, "private enterprise…manages so much better all the concerns to which it is equal," and Americans support a strong national defense, but not an overgrown military-industrial complex.*

Note: Theodore Roosevelt's quote at the beginning of this chapter should not be construed to mean that only English should be spoken in the USA. Rather, the quote means that English should be the official language of the USA, that persons desiring to become US citizens should be conversant in written and spoken English, and that the government should do its business in English. Fundamentally, being American comes down to equality before the law, and common sense. It is not feasible, practically or economically, for a country as large and diverse as the USA, to have multiple language versions of all its business – tax code, voting ballots, driving license test, etc. Yes, there are two official versions of everything in Canada, but that situation is based on there having been both English and French persons present in large numbers at the time of the founding of Canada. To make such an accommodation today in the USA, the government would have to have a Spanish, Hindi, Chinese, Korean,

Vietnamese, Japanese, Russian, and Arabic, and several other language, versions of its business.

The bottom line here is that diversity of languages, religions, and cultures, adds spice and interest to American societal fabric. But, for a person to prosper in American society and to not be a burden on the American taxpayers, a working knowledge of spoken and written English is necessary. All Americans' primary allegiance needs to be to our Judeo-Christian based moral and political system, and that system, in the USA, was born and developed in the English language.

So - if an immigrant "comes here in good faith, becomes an American and assimilates himself to us, he shall be treated on an exact equality with everyone else, for it is an outrage to discriminate against any such man because of creed, or birthplace, or origin."

What should these words mean for immigration? First, "good faith" should mean legally. But - it should also mean to come to the USA with the desire to follow the American political system as set up in the Constitution and to subscribe to the American Judeo-Christian value set.

What about all the illegal immigrants in the USA - have they all come here in good faith? Probably not, but here is where the Judeo-Christian value of compassion comes into play. First, let us all recognize that the USA cannot absorb an unlimited number of immigrants. The physical and financial strain on everything from healthcare to education would be too great to bear. Immigration law needs to be reformed immediately: first, control the borders; second, revise immigration laws to provide a controlled number of immigrants who increase "the wealth and strength of the community" (immigrants can increase the strength of a community by their hard work and moral values compatible with American values - immigrants don't have to be "rich" to provide "strength" to a community).

Third, for illegal immigrants (and their families) that have been present in the USA for a certain period (maybe two years?), that have worked hard, that do not have a felony or significant misdemeanor criminal record - for these people, Congress should pass a law with the following provisions: allows illegal immigrants (and their families), as described above, to admit their guilt for entering the country, to then be given a fine to pay ($2,000?), and to then be given a green card with employment *rights for ten years. Then, as with any other green card holder, they can apply for citizenship under the current rules.*

This proposal requires "justice under the law": it requires illegal immigrants to admit breaking the law (avoiding the grant of amnesty), and it provides a not insignificant penalty for that crime. This proposal demonstrates grace: This proposal shows that America is not blind to the desire of the "tired... poor...huddled masses yearning to breathe free, the wretched refuse" of the world's population, to find a better way of life, to find a better future for their children and grandchildren. Is that desire not the desire of every good parent and grandparent on earth? If the answer is yes, Americans need to show grace to the illegal immigrant "criminals" who have come to our shores to truly integrate into our society and to accept America's moral, political, and economic system – as laid out in this book's interviews. Americans – we must show mercy to illegal immigrants.

"The quality of mercy is not strained,
It droppeth as the gentle rain from heaven upon the place beneath.
It is twice blest,
It blesseth him that gives, and him that takes,
'Tis mightiest in the mightiest, it becomes
The throned Monarch better than his Crown.
His Scepter shows the force of temporal power,
The attribute to awe and Majesty,
Wherein doth sit the dread and fear of Kings.
But mercy is above this sceptered sway,
It is enthroned in the hearts of Kings,
It is an attribute to God himself;
And earthly power doth then show likest God's
When mercy seasons Justice"

<ins>The Merchant of Venice</ins>, Act IV, Scene 1, Shakespeare
(Quoted from a Gutenberg Project public domain copy of this play)

A final thought on immigration, if Shakespeare's appeal for mercy did not appeal to you. Remember, no matter the color of your skin, your gender, or your country of origin, all persons have equal worth. I'll turn to Shakespeare one more time to beautifully drive this point home:

Hath not the minority[19] eyes?
Hath not
the minority hands?
Organs, dimensions, senses,
affections, passions?
Fed with the same food, hurt
with the same weapons,
subject to the same diseases,
healed by the same
means, warmed and cooled by
the same winter and
summer as the majority?
If you prick them do they not
bleed? If you tickle them, do
they not laugh? If you poison
them, do they not die?

The Merchant of Venice, Act III, Scene 1, Shakespeare
(Quoted from a Gutenberg Project public domain copy of this play)

---

[19] In the original, "minority" is actually "Jew." You can substitute any gender, race, or skin color between the quotation marks, but the point is the same: human nature is constant, and all human life deserves an equal measure of respect.

CHAPTER 6

FINAL THOUGHTS - ON GUNS AND BUTTER

"From my cold, dead hands"[20]

MOD: Gentlemen, I am grateful for the time and insight you have provided today. Your experience and wisdom have no parallel in American history, and all Americans, and the world for that matter, would do well to heed your counsel, warnings, and admonishments. I have a few more topics to discuss that, I hope, will not be too lengthy. First, let us start with the Constitution's Second Amendment: "A well-regulated militia, being necessary to the security of a free state, the right of the people to keep and bear arms shall not be infringed." Gentlemen, what did you mean by these words?

JM: I wrote in "Federalist 46" that "the advantage of being armed, which the Americans possess over the people of almost every other nation… forms a barrier against the enterprises of ambition [of government], more insurmountable than any which a simple government of any form can admit of…the several kingdoms of Europe…are afraid to trust the people with arms."

---

[20] Charlton Heston, referring to any attempt by the government to nullify his right to bear arms.

MOD: President Madison, it appears you believe that an armed citizenry provides a defense against "the enterprises of ambition" of the federal government. Do you mean by "enterprises of ambition" forceful actions by the federal government to usurp power not granted to it under the Constitution and to take citizens' property without due process of law?

JM: I will let the words speak for themselves.

MOD: And do you believe that Americans bearing arms is an advantage for the USA?

JM: I did say that bearing arms is an advantage for the American people.

MOD: You seem to indicate that the centralized, tyrannical governments of 18th century Europe feared an armed citizenry because an armed citizenry could rise up against tyranny? Should the American government trust its citizens with firearms?

JM: I believe that a few of my fellow revolutionary patriots who could not be here with us today can provide a concise and straightforward answer to the question you pose. Let me start with Samuel Adams, member of the Continental Congress in 1776 at the time of the Declaration of Independence and cousin of President Adams, who said during the Massachusetts constitutional ratifying convention that the "Constitution [should] be never construed to authorize Congress to infringe the just liberty of the press, or the rights of conscience; or to prevent the people of the United States, who are peaceable citizens, *from keeping their own arms* [emphasis added]."

Additionally, the eminent scholar and editor of *The Federalist Papers*, Noah Webster, stated that "before a standing army can rule, the people must be disarmed; as they are in almost every kingdom in Europe. The supreme power in America cannot enforce unjust laws by the sword; because the whole body of the people are armed, and constitute a force superior to any band of regular troops that can be, on any pretense, raised in the United States."

Finally, George Mason, another well respected patriot and delegate to the Constitutional Convention, reminded us all in his 1788 address to the Virginia Constitutional Ratifying convention that "Forty years ago, when the resolution of enslaving America was formed in Great Britain, the British parliament was advised by an artful man, [Sir William Keith], who was governor of Pennsylvania, to disarm the people....it was the best and most effectual way to enslave them."[21]

MOD: Seems pretty clear that you, President Madison, and your fellow patriots believed strongly in the right of citizens to bear arms and that the Second Amendment was indeed meant to preserve and protect the right of the citizenry to keep and bear arms. Thank you President Madison for recalling these important and timely points.

Finally, on a lighter note, contemporary Americans are facing a big – and yes my pun is intended – problem – that of increasing obesity and unhealthiness among the populace. I know you, Mr. Franklin said, "To lengthen thy life, lessen they meals" and "Early to bed and early to rise makes a man healthy, wealthy, and wise." Does our panel have any other comments on this issue?

TJ: It is well known that I was a life-long learner, so much so that after the British army burned the Library of Congress in 1814 during the War of 1812, I sold my personal library of over 6,000 books to the Library of Congress to replenish its shelves. Yet, I've always said that "Give about two of them [hours] every day to exercise; for health must not be sacrificed to learning. A strong body makes the mind strong. As to the species of exercise, I advise the gun. While this gives a moderate exercise to the body, it gives boldness, enterprise, and independence to the mind. Games played with the ball and others of that nature, are too violent for the body and stamp no character on the mind. Let your gun therefore be the constant companion of your walks. Never think of taking a book with you. The object of walking is to relax the mind. You should therefore not permit yourself even to think while you walk. But divert your attention by the objects surrounding you. Walking is the best possible exercise. Habituate yourself to walk very far. The Europeans value themselves on having subdued the horse to the uses of man. But I doubt whether we have not lost more than we have gained by the use of this animal. No one has occasioned so much the degeneracy of the human body. An Indian goes on foot nearly as far in a day, for a

---

[21]   George Mason, speech in the Virginia Ratifying Convention, 1788

long journey, as an enfeebled white does on his horse, and he will tire the best horses. There is no habit you will value so much as that of walking far without fatigue. I would advise you to take your exercise in the afternoon. Not because it is the best time for exercise for certainly it is not: but because it is the best time to spare from your studies; and habit will soon reconcile it to health, and render it nearly as useful as if you gave to that the more precious hours of the day. A little walk of half an hour in the morning when you first rise is advisable also. It shakes off sleep, and produces other good effects in the animal economy. Rise at a fixed and an early hour, and go to bed at a fixed and early hour also. Sitting up late at night is injurious to the health, and not useful to the mind."

And finally, since we have spent much of our day speaking on the role of government, and since we have now turned our dialogue to the topic of health, let me recall my astute observation on food, medicine, and the government: "Was the government to prescribe to us our medicine and diet, our bodies would be in such keeping as our souls are now.[22]"

End of this interview

Key quotes:

The "Constitution [should] be never construed to authorize Congress to infringe the just liberty of the press, or the rights of conscience; or to prevent the people of the United States, who are peaceable citizens, from keeping their own arms." Samuel Adams

"The advantage of being armed, which the Americans possess over the people of almost every other nation…forms a barrier against the enterprises of ambition [of government]." Madison

---

[22] What Jefferson means here is that in general, our souls are in a sorry state – ergo his admonition to take charge of our own diet and health and to keep the government out of this arena. For a startling look into just how much control the federal government has over citizens' attempts to control their diet and their food buying habits, watch the film *Farmageddon – The Unseen War On American Family Farms* ©2011.

Moderator's Notes: *First, I was amazed, and pleased, to see that Jefferson even foresaw that an ever expanding federal government would eventually try to control citizen's decisions about the food they eat and the medicine they take. Yep, we're there – watch the movie noted in footnote 22.*

How about the Founders' personal habits? Well, you just read some advice from Jefferson on this topic – talk a walk, get some exercise, clear your mind. But how did these men spend their time? Well, here's how Franklin spent his days. If you're looking for a daily routine, you might start here, because Franklin must certainly be considered to be one of the most productive Americans, based on his extensive government service, charitable work, and scientific research:

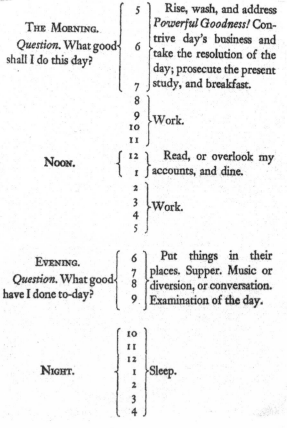

THE MORNING. Question. What good shall I do this day?	5 6 7	Rise, wash, and address *Powerful Goodness!* Contrive day's business and take the resolution of the day; prosecute the present study, and breakfast.
	8 9 10 11	Work.
NOON.	12 1	Read, or overlook my accounts, and dine.
	2 3 4 5	Work.
EVENING. Question. What good have I done to-day?	6 7 8 9	Put things in their places. Supper. Music or diversion, or conversation. Examination of the day.
NIGHT.	10 11 12 1 2 3 4	Sleep.

I suppose the only thing I would add is to exercise most days of the week, as Jefferson suggested.

As regards the Second Amendment, the right to bear arms, I had always been intellectually in favor of the right to bear arms. Then, I learned that American federal courts have repeatedly declared that law enforcement agencies have no legal obligation to respond to citizens' request for assistance when their life and/or property are threatened. Now, I am a fervent advocate of the Second Amendment, and I would suggest to all Americans that they make provisions for their own protection, to include a firearm if so inclined, because the bad guys are usually armed – so you better be too – no government authority is legally obligated to come to your aid when the bad guys threaten you. If you wish to explore this idea further, do research on these legal cases: Warren v. District of Columbia, and Castle Rock v. Gonzales.

AFTERWORD

In closing, as An American, I pray that God may give American citizens the wisdom to see the numerous and dangerous threats to their way of life, and to fervently, and peaceably, use the power of the ballot box, of freedom of speech, of religion, and of the press, to repel these dangers, before the lamp of liberty is forever extinguished from American shores.

Oh America! "May the Lord bless you and keep you,
May He make his face to shine upon you,
May He give you prosperity and peace."**

America, you are the great hope for the world,
The light atop the hill of liberty,
The beacon on the shores of prosperity,
May you and your people always remember,
God has "shed his grace on thee,
And crowned thy good, with brotherhood,
From sea to sea shining sea."

**Numbers 6:24-26

PRESIDENT GEORGE WASHINGTON'S
FAREWELL ADDRESS
(Procured with gratitude from the Lillian Goldman Law Library)

Moderator's Note: This document, in my educated and informed opinion, is the definitive guide post for American politics and society. If Americans were to comport themselves with Washington's recommendations for personal virtue, and if American politicians were to comport themselves with Washington's counsel concerning finances, foreign affairs, and party politics, America would quickly emerge from its current state of economic stagnation and moral decline. By the way, this "address" was published in written form. It was not a speech.

To the PEOPLE of the UNITED STATES:
19 September, 1796
Friends and Citizens:

The period for a new election of a citizen to administer the executive government of the United States being not far distant, and the time actually arrived when your thoughts must be employed in designating the person who is to be clothed with that important trust, it appears to me proper, especially as it may conduce to a more distinct expression of the public voice, that I should now apprise you of the resolution I have formed, to decline being considered among the number of those out of whom a choice is to be made.

I beg you, at the same time, to do me the justice to be assured that this resolution has not been taken without a strict regard to all the considerations appertaining to the relation which binds a dutiful citizen to his country; and that in withdrawing the tender of service, which silence in my situation might imply, I am influenced by no diminution of zeal for your future interest, no deficiency of grateful respect for your past kindness, but am supported by a full conviction that the step is compatible with both.

The acceptance of, and continuance hitherto in, the office to which your suffrages have twice called me have been a uniform sacrifice of inclination to the opinion of duty and to a deference for what appeared to be your desire. I constantly hoped that it would have been much earlier in my power, consistently with motives which I was not at liberty to disregard, to return to that retirement from which I had been reluctantly drawn. The strength of my inclination to do this, previous to the last election, had even led to the preparation of an address to declare it to you; but mature reflection on the then perplexed and critical posture of our affairs with foreign nations, and the unanimous advice of persons entitled to my confidence, impelled me to abandon the idea.

I rejoice that the state of your concerns, external as well as internal, no longer renders the pursuit of inclination incompatible with the sentiment of duty or propriety, and am persuaded, whatever partiality may be retained for my services, that, in the present circumstances of our country, you will not disapprove my determination to retire.

The impressions with which I first undertook the arduous trust were explained on the proper occasion. In the discharge of this trust, I will only say that I have, with good intentions, contributed towards the organization and administration of the government the best exertions of which a very fallible judgment was capable. Not unconscious in the outset of the inferiority of my qualifications, experience in my own eyes, perhaps still more in the eyes of others, has strengthened the motives to diffidence [hesitancy] of myself; and every day the increasing weight of years admonishes me more and more that the shade of retirement is as necessary to me as it will be welcome. Satisfied that if any circumstances have given peculiar value to my services, they were temporary, I have the consolation to believe that, while choice and prudence invite me to quit the political scene, patriotism does not forbid it.

In looking forward to the moment which is intended to terminate the career of my public life, my feelings do not permit me to suspend the deep acknowledgment of that debt of gratitude which I owe to my beloved country for the many honors it has conferred upon me; still more for the steadfast confidence with which it has supported me; and for the opportunities I have thence enjoyed of manifesting my inviolable attachment, by services faithful and persevering, though in usefulness unequal to my zeal. If benefits have resulted to our country from these services, let it always be remembered to your praise, and as an instructive example in our annals, that under circumstances in which the passions, agitated in every direction, were liable to mislead, amidst appearances sometimes dubious, vicissitudes of fortune often discouraging, in situations in which not unfrequently want of success has countenanced the spirit of criticism, the constancy of your support was the essential prop of the efforts, and a guarantee of the plans by which they were effected. Profoundly penetrated with this idea, I shall carry it with me to my grave, as a strong incitement to unceasing vows that heaven may continue to you the choicest tokens of its beneficence; that your union and brotherly affection may be perpetual; that the free Constitution, which is the work of your hands, may be sacredly maintained; that its administration in every department may be stamped with wisdom and virtue; that, in fine, the happiness of the people of these States, under the auspices of liberty, may be made complete by so careful a preservation and so prudent a use of this blessing as will acquire to them the glory of recommending it to the applause, the affection, and adoption of every nation which is yet a stranger to it.

Here, perhaps, I ought to stop. But a solicitude for your welfare, which cannot end but with my life, and the apprehension of danger, natural to that solicitude, urge me, on an occasion like the present, to offer to your solemn contemplation, and to recommend to your frequent review, some sentiments which are the result of much reflection, of no inconsiderable observation, and which appear to me all-important to the permanency of your felicity as a people. These will be offered to you with the more freedom, as you can only see in them the disinterested warnings of a parting friend, who can possibly have no personal motive to bias his counsel. Nor can I forget, as an encouragement to it, your indulgent reception of my sentiments on a former and not dissimilar occasion.

Interwoven as is the love of liberty with every ligament of your hearts, no recommendation of mine is necessary to fortify or confirm the attachment.

The unity of government which constitutes you one people is also now dear to you. It is justly so, for it is a main pillar in the edifice of your real independence, the support of your tranquility at home, your peace abroad; of your safety; of your prosperity; of that very liberty which you so highly prize. But as it is easy to foresee that, from different causes and from different quarters, much pains will be taken, many artifices employed to weaken in your minds the conviction of this truth; as this is the point in *your political fortress against which the batteries of internal and external enemies will be most constantly and actively (though often covertly and insidiously) directed, it is of infinite moment that you should properly estimate the immense value of your national union to your collective and individual happiness; that you should cherish a cordial, habitual, and immovable attachment to it; accustoming yourselves to think and speak of it as of the palladium of your political safety and prosperity; watching for its preservation with jealous anxiety; discountenancing whatever may suggest even a suspicion that it can in any event be abandoned; and indignantly frowning upon the first dawning of every attempt to alienate any portion of our country from the rest, or to enfeeble the sacred ties which now link together the various parts.*

For this you have every inducement of sympathy and interest. Citizens, by birth or choice, of a common country, that country has a right to concentrate your affections. The name of American, which belongs to you in your national capacity, must always exalt the just pride of patriotism more than any appellation derived from local discriminations. With slight shades of difference, you have the same religion, manners, habits, and political principles. You have in a common cause fought and triumphed together; the independence and liberty you possess are the work of joint counsels, and joint efforts of common dangers, sufferings, and successes.

But these considerations, however powerfully they address themselves to your sensibility, are greatly outweighed by those which apply more immediately to your interest. Here every portion of our country finds the most commanding motives for carefully guarding and preserving the union of the whole.

The North, in an unrestrained intercourse with the South, protected by the equal laws of a common government, finds in the productions of the latter great additional resources of maritime and commercial enterprise and precious materials of manufacturing industry. The South, in the same intercourse, benefiting by the agency of the North, sees its agriculture grow and its commerce expand. Turning partly into its own channels the seamen of the North, it finds its particular navigation invigorated; and, while it contributes, in different ways, to nourish and increase the general mass of the national navigation, it looks forward to the protection of a maritime strength, to which itself is unequally adapted. The East, in a like intercourse with the West, already finds, and in the progressive improvement of interior communications by land and water, will more and more find a valuable vent for the commodities which it brings from abroad, or manufactures at home. The West derives from the East supplies requisite to its growth and comfort, and, what is perhaps of still greater consequence, it must of necessity owe the secure enjoyment of indispensable outlets for its own productions to the weight, influence, and the future maritime strength of the Atlantic side of the Union, directed by an indissoluble community of interest as one nation. Any other tenure, by which the West can hold this essential advantage, whether derived from its own separate strength, or from an apostate and unnatural connection with any foreign power, must be intrinsically precarious.

While, then, every part of our country thus feels an immediate and particular interest in union, all the parts combined cannot fail to find in the united mass of means and efforts greater strength, greater resource, proportionally greater security from external danger, a less frequent interruption of their peace by foreign nations; and, what is of inestimable value, they must derive from union an exemption from those broils and wars between themselves, which so frequently afflict neighboring countries not tied together by the same governments, which their own rival ships alone would be sufficient to produce, but which opposite foreign alliances, attachments, and intrigues would stimulate and embitter. Hence, likewise, they will avoid the necessity of those overgrown military establishments which, under any form of government, are inauspicious to liberty, and which are to be regarded as particularly hostile to republican liberty. In this sense it is that your union ought to be considered as a main prop of your liberty, and that the love of the one ought to endear to you the preservation of the other.

These considerations speak a persuasive language to every reflecting and virtuous mind, and exhibit the continuance of the Union as a primary object of patriotic desire. Is there a doubt whether a common government can embrace so large a sphere? Let experience solve it. To listen to mere speculation in such a case were criminal. We are authorized to hope that a proper organization of the whole with the auxiliary agency of governments for the respective subdivisions, will afford a happy issue to the experiment. It is well worth a fair and full experiment. With such powerful and obvious motives to union, affecting all parts of our country, while experience shall not have demonstrated its impracticability, there will always be reason to distrust the patriotism of those who in any quarter may endeavor to weaken its bands.

In contemplating the causes which may disturb our Union, it occurs as matter of serious concern that any ground should have been furnished for characterizing parties by geographical discriminations, Northern and Southern, Atlantic and Western; whence designing men may endeavor to excite a belief that there is a real difference of local interests and views. One of the expedients of party to acquire influence within particular districts is to misrepresent the opinions and aims of other districts. You cannot shield yourselves too much against the jealousies and heartburnings which spring from these misrepresentations; they tend to render alien to each other those who ought to be bound together by fraternal affection. The inhabitants of our Western country have lately had a useful lesson on this head; they have seen, in the negotiation by the Executive, and in the unanimous ratification by the Senate, of the treaty with Spain, and in the universal satisfaction at that event, throughout the United States, a decisive proof how unfounded were the suspicions propagated among them of a policy in the General Government and in the Atlantic States unfriendly to their interests in regard to the Mississippi; they have been witnesses to the formation of two treaties, that with Great Britain, and that with Spain, which secure to them everything they could desire, in respect to our foreign relations, towards confirming their prosperity. Will it not be their wisdom to rely for the preservation of these advantages on the Union by which they were procured? Will they not henceforth be deaf to those advisers, if such there are, who would sever them from their brethren and connect them with aliens?

To the efficacy and permanency of your Union, a government for the whole is indispensable. No alliance, however strict, between the parts can be an adequate substitute; they must inevitably experience the infractions and interruptions which all alliances in all times have experienced. Sensible of this momentous truth, you have improved upon your first essay, by the adoption of a constitution of government better calculated than your former for an intimate union, and for the efficacious management of your common concerns. This government, the offspring of our own choice, uninfluenced and unawed, adopted upon full investigation and mature deliberation, completely free in its principles, in the distribution of its powers, uniting security with energy, and containing within itself a provision for its own amendment, has a just claim to your confidence and your support. Respect for its authority, compliance with its laws, acquiescence in its measures, are duties enjoined by the fundamental maxims of true liberty. The basis of our political systems is the right of the people to make and to alter their constitutions of government. But the Constitution which at any time exists, till changed by an explicit and authentic act of the whole people, is sacredly obligatory upon all. The very idea of the power and the right of the people to establish government presupposes the duty of every individual to obey the established government.

All obstructions to the execution of the laws, all combinations and associations, under whatever plausible character, with the real design to direct, control, counteract, or awe the regular deliberation and action of the constituted authorities, are destructive of this fundamental principle, and of fatal tendency. They serve to organize faction, to give it an artificial and extraordinary force; to put, in the place of the delegated will of the nation the will of a party, often a small but artful and enterprising minority of the community; and, according to the alternate triumphs of different parties, to make the public administration the mirror of the ill-concerted and incongruous projects of faction, rather than the organ of consistent and wholesome plans digested by common counsels and modified by mutual interests.

However combinations or associations of the above description may now and then answer popular ends, they are likely, in the course of time and things, to become potent engines, by which cunning, ambitious, and unprincipled men will be enabled to subvert the power of the people and to usurp for themselves the reins of government, destroying afterwards the very engines which have lifted them to unjust dominion.

Towards the preservation of your government, and the permanency of your present happy state, it is requisite, not only that you steadily discountenance irregular oppositions to its acknowledged authority, but also that you resist with care the spirit of innovation upon its principles, however specious the pretexts. One method of assault may be to effect, in *the forms of the Constitution, alterations which will impair the energy of the system, and thus to undermine what cannot be directly overthrown. In all the changes to which you may be invited, remember that time and habit are at least as necessary to fix the true character of governments as of other human institutions; that experience is the surest standard by which to test the real tendency of the existing constitution of a country; that facility in changes, upon the credit of mere hypothesis and opinion, exposes to perpetual change, from the endless variety of hypothesis and opinion; and remember, especially, that for the efficient management of your common interests, in a country so extensive as ours, a government of as much vigor as is consistent with the perfect security of liberty is indispensable. Liberty itself will find in such a government, with powers properly distributed and adjusted, its surest guardian. It is, indeed, little else than a name, where the government is too feeble to withstand the enterprises of faction, to confine each member of the society within the limits prescribed by the laws, and to maintain all in the secure and tranquil enjoyment of the rights of person and property.*

I have already intimated to you the danger of parties in the State, with particular reference to the founding of them on geographical discriminations. Let me now take a more comprehensive view, and warn you in the most solemn manner against the baneful effects of the spirit of party generally.

This spirit, unfortunately, is inseparable from our nature, having its root in the strongest passions of the human mind. It exists under different shapes in all governments, more or less stifled, controlled, or repressed; but, in those of the popular form, it is seen in its greatest rankness, and is truly their worst enemy.

The alternate domination of one faction over another, sharpened by the spirit of revenge, natural to party dissension, which in different ages and countries has perpetrated the most horrid enormities, is itself a frightful despotism. But this leads at length to a more formal and permanent despotism. The disorders and miseries which result gradually incline the minds of men to seek security and repose in the absolute power of an individual; and sooner or later the chief of some prevailing faction, more able or more fortunate than his competitors, turns this disposition to the purposes of his own elevation, on the ruins of public liberty.

Without looking forward to an extremity of this kind (which nevertheless ought not to be entirely out of sight), the common and continual mischiefs of the spirit of party are sufficient to make it the interest and duty of a wise people to discourage and restrain it.

It serves always to distract the public councils and enfeeble the public administration. It agitates the community with ill-founded jealousies and false alarms, kindles the animosity of one part against another, and foments occasionally riot and insurrection. It opens the door to foreign influence and corruption, which finds a facilitated access to the government itself through the channels of party passions. Thus the policy and the will of one country are subjected to the policy and will of another.

There is an opinion that parties in free countries are useful checks upon the administration of the government and serve to keep alive the spirit of liberty. This within certain limits is probably true; and in governments of a monarchical cast, patriotism may look with indulgence, if not with favor, upon the spirit of party. But in those of the popular character, in governments purely elective, it is a spirit not to be encouraged. From their natural tendency, it is certain there will always be enough of that spirit for every salutary purpose. And there being constant danger of excess, the effort ought to be by force of public opinion, to mitigate and assuage it. A fire not to be quenched, it demands a uniform vigilance to prevent its bursting into a flame, lest, instead of warming, it should consume.

It is important, likewise, that the habits of thinking in a free country should inspire caution in those entrusted with its administration, to confine themselves within their respective constitutional spheres, avoiding in the exercise of the powers of one department to encroach upon another. The spirit of encroachment tends to consolidate the powers of all the departments in one, and thus to create, whatever the form of government, a real despotism. A just estimate of that love of power, and proneness to abuse it, which predominates in the human heart, is sufficient to satisfy us of the truth of this position. The necessity of reciprocal checks in the exercise of political power, by dividing and distributing it into different depositaries, and constituting each the guardian of the public weal against invasions by the others, has been evinced by experiments ancient and modern; some of them in our country and under our own eyes. To preserve them must be as necessary as to institute them. If, in the opinion of the people, the distribution or modification of the constitutional powers be in any particular wrong, let it be corrected by an amendment in the way which the Constitution designates. But let there be no change by usurpation; for though this, in one instance, may be the instrument of good, it is the customary weapon by which free governments are destroyed. The precedent must always greatly overbalance in permanent evil any partial or transient benefit, which the use can at any time yield.

Of all the dispositions and habits which lead to political prosperity, religion and morality are indispensable supports. In vain would that man claim the tribute of patriotism, who should labor to subvert these great pillars of human happiness, these firmest props of the duties of men and citizens. The mere politician, equally with the pious man, ought to respect and to cherish them. A volume could not trace all their connections with private and public felicity. Let it simply be asked: Where is the security for property, for reputation, for life, if the sense of religious obligation deserts the oaths which are the instruments of investigation in courts of justice? And let us with caution indulge the supposition that morality can be maintained without religion. Whatever may be conceded to the influence of refined education on minds of peculiar structure, reason and experience both forbid us to expect that national morality can prevail in exclusion of religious principle.

It is substantially true that virtue or morality is a necessary spring of popular government. The rule, indeed, extends with more or less force to every species of free government. Who that is a sincere friend to it can look with indifference upon attempts to shake the foundation of the fabric?

Promote then, as an object of primary importance, institutions for the general diffusion of knowledge. In proportion as the structure of a government gives force to public opinion, it is essential that public opinion should be enlightened.

As a very important source of strength and security, cherish public credit. One method of preserving it is to use it as sparingly as possible, avoiding occasions of expense by cultivating peace, but remembering also that timely disbursements to prepare for danger frequently prevent much greater disbursements to repel it, avoiding likewise the accumulation of debt, not only by shunning occasions of expense, but by vigorous exertion in time of peace to discharge the debts which unavoidable wars may have occasioned, not ungenerously throwing upon posterity the burden which we ourselves ought to bear. The execution of these maxims belongs to your representatives, but it is necessary that public opinion should co-operate. To facilitate to them the performance of their duty, it is essential that you should practically bear in mind that towards the payment of debts there must be revenue; that to have revenue there must be taxes; that no taxes can be devised which are not more or less inconvenient and unpleasant; that the intrinsic embarrassment, inseparable from the selection of the proper objects (which is always a choice of difficulties), ought to be a decisive motive for a candid construction of the conduct of the government in making it, and for a spirit of acquiescence in the measures for obtaining revenue, which the public exigencies may at any time dictate.

Observe good faith and justice towards all nations; cultivate peace and harmony with all. Religion and morality enjoin this conduct; and can it be, that good policy does not equally enjoin it - It will be worthy of a free, enlightened, and at no distant period, a great nation, to give to mankind the magnanimous and too novel example of a people always guided by an exalted justice and benevolence. Who can doubt that, in the course of time and things, the fruits of such a plan would richly repay any temporary advantages which might be lost by a steady adherence to it? Can it be that Providence has not connected the permanent felicity of a nation with its virtue? The experiment, at least, is recommended by every sentiment which ennobles human nature. Alas! Is it rendered impossible by its vices?

In the execution of such a plan, nothing is more essential than that permanent, inveterate antipathies [constant antagonism] against particular nations, and passionate attachments for others, should be excluded; and that, in place of them, just and amicable feelings towards all should be cultivated. The nation which indulges towards another a habitual hatred or a habitual fondness is in some degree a slave. It is a slave to its animosity or to its affection, either of which is sufficient to lead it astray from its duty and its interest. Antipathy in one nation against another disposes each more readily to offer insult and injury, to lay hold of slight causes of umbrage, and to be haughty and intractable, when accidental or trifling occasions of dispute occur. Hence, frequent collisions, obstinate, envenomed, and bloody contests. The nation, prompted by ill-will and resentment, sometimes impels to war the government, contrary to the best calculations of policy. The government sometimes participates in the national propensity, and adopts through passion what reason would reject; at other times it makes the animosity of the nation subservient to projects of hostility instigated by pride, ambition, and other sinister and pernicious motives. The peace often, sometimes perhaps the liberty, of nations, has been the victim.

So likewise, a passionate attachment of one nation for another produces a variety of evils. Sympathy for the favorite nation, facilitating the illusion of an imaginary common interest in cases where no real common interest exists, and infusing into one the enmities of the other, betrays the former into a participation in the quarrels and wars of the latter without adequate inducement or justification. It leads also to concessions to the favorite nation of privileges denied to others which is apt doubly to injure the nation making the concessions; by unnecessarily parting with what ought to have been retained, and by exciting jealousy, ill-will, and a disposition to retaliate, in the parties from whom equal privileges are withheld. And it gives to ambitious, corrupted, or deluded citizens (who devote themselves to the favorite nation), facility to betray or sacrifice the interests of their own country, without odium, sometimes even with popularity; gilding, with the appearances of a virtuous sense of obligation, a commendable deference for public opinion, or a laudable zeal for public good, the base or foolish compliances of ambition, corruption, or infatuation.

As avenues to foreign influence in innumerable ways, such attachments are particularly alarming to the truly enlightened and independent patriot. How many opportunities do they afford to tamper with domestic factions, to practice the arts of seduction, to mislead public opinion, to influence or awe the public councils. Such an attachment of a small or weak towards a great and powerful nation dooms the former to be the satellite of the latter.

Against the insidious wiles of foreign influence (I conjure you to believe me, fellow-citizens) the jealousy of a free people ought to be constantly awake, since history and experience prove that foreign influence is one of the most baneful foes of republican government. But that jealousy to be useful must be impartial; else it becomes the instrument of the very *influence to be avoided, instead of a defense against it. Excessive partiality for one foreign nation and excessive dislike of another cause those whom they actuate to see danger only on one side, and serve to veil and even second the arts of influence on the other. Real patriots who may resist the intrigues of the favorite are liable to become suspected and odious, while its tools and dupes usurp the applause and confidence of the people, to surrender their interests.*

The great rule of conduct for us in regard to foreign nations is in extending our commercial relations, to have with them as little political connection as possible. So far as we have already formed engagements, let them be fulfilled with perfect good faith. Here let us stop. Europe has a set of primary interests which to us have none; or a very remote relation. Hence she must be engaged in frequent controversies, the causes of which are essentially foreign to our concerns. Hence, therefore, it must be unwise in us to implicate ourselves by artificial ties in the ordinary vicissitudes of her politics, or the ordinary combinations and collisions of her friendships or enmities.

Our detached and distant situation invites and enables us to pursue a different course. If we remain one people under an efficient government, the period is not far off when we may defy material injury from external annoyance; when we may take such an attitude as will cause the neutrality we may at any time resolve upon to be scrupulously respected; when belligerent nations, under the impossibility of making acquisitions upon us, will not lightly hazard the giving us provocation; when we may choose peace or war, as our interest, guided by justice, shall counsel.

Why forego the advantages of so peculiar a situation? Why quit our own to stand upon foreign ground? Why, by interweaving our destiny with that of any part of Europe, entangle our peace and prosperity in the toils of European ambition, rivalship [rivalry], interest, humor or caprice?

It is our true policy to steer clear of permanent alliances with any portion of the foreign world; so far, I mean, as we are now at liberty to do it; for let me not be understood as capable of patronizing infidelity to existing engagements. I hold the maxim no less applicable to public than to private affairs, that honesty is always the best policy. I repeat it, therefore, let those engagements be observed in their genuine sense. But, in my opinion, it is unnecessary and would be unwise to extend them.

Taking care always to keep ourselves by suitable establishments on a respectable defensive posture, we may safely trust to temporary alliances for extraordinary emergencies.

Harmony, liberal intercourse with all nations, are recommended by policy, humanity, and interest. But even our commercial policy should hold an equal and impartial hand; neither seeking nor granting exclusive favors or preferences; consulting the natural course of things; diffusing and diversifying by gentle means the streams of commerce, but forcing nothing; establishing (with powers so disposed, in order to give trade a stable course, to define the rights of our merchants, and to enable the government to support them) conventional rules of intercourse, the best that present circumstances and mutual opinion will permit, but temporary, and liable to be from time to time abandoned or varied, as experience and circumstances shall dictate; constantly keeping in view that it is folly in one nation to look for disinterested favors from another; that it must pay with a portion of its independence for whatever it may accept under that character; that, by such acceptance, it may place itself in the condition of having given equivalents for nominal favors, and yet of being reproached with ingratitude for not giving more. There can be no greater error than to expect or calculate upon real favors from nation to nation. It is an illusion, which experience must cure, which a just pride ought to discard.

In offering to you, my countrymen, these counsels of an old and affectionate friend, I dare not hope they will make the strong and lasting impression I could wish; that they will control the usual current of the passions, or prevent our nation from running the course which has hitherto marked the destiny of nations. But, if I may even flatter myself that they may be productive of some partial benefit, some occasional good; that they may now and then recur to moderate the fury of party spirit, to warn against the mischiefs of foreign intrigue, to guard against the impostures of pretended patriotism; this hope will be a full recompense for the solicitude for your welfare, by which they have been dictated.

How far in the discharge of my official duties I have been guided by the principles which have been delineated, the public records and other evidences of my conduct must witness to you and to the world. To myself, the assurance of my own conscience is, that I have at least believed myself to be guided by them.

In relation to the still subsisting war in Europe, my proclamation of the twenty-second of April, 1793, is the index of my plan. Sanctioned by your approving voice, and by that of your representatives in both houses of Congress, the spirit of that measure has continually governed me, uninfluenced by any attempts to deter or divert me from it.

After deliberate examination, with the aid of the best lights I could obtain, I was well satisfied that our country, under all the circumstances of the case, had a right to take, and was bound in duty and interest to take, a neutral position. Having taken it, I determined, as far as should depend upon me, to maintain it, with moderation, perseverance, and firmness.

The considerations which respect the right to hold this conduct, it is not necessary on this occasion to detail. I will only observe that, according to my understanding of the matter, that right, so far from being denied by any of the belligerent powers, has been virtually admitted by all.

The duty of holding a neutral conduct may be inferred, without anything more, from the obligation which justice and humanity impose on every nation, in cases in which it is free to act, to maintain inviolate the relations of peace and amity towards other nations.

The inducements of interest for observing that conduct will best be referred to your own reflections and experience. With me a predominant motive has been to endeavor to gain time to our country to settle and mature its yet recent institutions, and to progress without interruption to that degree of strength and consistency which is necessary to give it, humanly speaking, the command of its own fortunes.

Though, in reviewing the incidents of my administration, I am unconscious of intentional error, I am nevertheless too sensible of my defects not to think it probable that I may have committed many errors. Whatever they may be, I fervently beseech the Almighty to avert or mitigate the evils to which they may tend. I shall also carry with me the hope that my country will never cease to view them with indulgence; and that, after forty five years of my life dedicated to its service with an upright zeal, the faults of incompetent abilities will be consigned to oblivion, as myself must soon be to the mansions of rest.

Relying on its kindness in this as in other things, and actuated by that fervent love towards it, which is so natural to a man who views in it the native soil of himself and his progenitors for several generations,

I anticipate with pleasing expectation that retreat in which I promise myself to realize, without alloy, the sweet enjoyment of partaking, in the midst of my fellow-citizens, the benign influence of good laws under a free government, the ever-favorite object of my heart, and the happy reward, as I trust, of our mutual cares, labors, and dangers.

G. WASHINGTON

THOMAS JEFFERSON'S FIRST
INAUGURAL ADDRESS
(Procured with gratitude from the Lillian Goldman Law Library)

March 4, 1801
FRIENDS AND FELLOW-CITIZENS,

Called upon to undertake the duties of the first executive office of our country, I avail myself of the presence of that portion of my fellow-citizens which is here assembled to express my grateful thanks for the favor with which they have been pleased to look toward me, to declare a sincere consciousness that the task is above my talents, and that I approach it with those anxious and awful presentiments which the greatness of the charge and the weakness of my powers so justly inspire. A rising nation, spread over a wide and fruitful land, traversing all the seas with the rich productions of their industry, engaged in commerce with nations who feel power and forget right, advancing rapidly to destinies beyond the reach of mortal eye -- when I contemplate these transcendent objects, and see the honor, the happiness, and the hopes of this beloved country committed to the issue and the auspices of this day, I shrink from the contemplation, and humble myself before the magnitude of the undertaking. Utterly, indeed, should I despair did not the presence of many whom I here see remind me that in the other high authorities provided by our Constitution I shall find resources of wisdom, of virtue, and of zeal on which to rely under all difficulties. To you, then, gentlemen, who are charged with the sovereign functions of legislation, and to those associated with you, I look with encouragement for that guidance and support which may enable us to steer with safety the vessel in which we are all embarked amidst the conflicting elements of a troubled world.

During the contest of opinion through which we have passed the animation of discussions and of exertions has sometimes worn an aspect which might impose on strangers unused to think freely and to speak and to write what they think; but this being now decided by the voice of the nation, announced according to the rules of the Constitution, all will, of course, arrange themselves under the will of the law, and unite in common efforts for the common good. All, too, will bear in mind this sacred principle, that though the will of the majority is in all cases to prevail, that will to be rightful must be reasonable; that the minority possess their equal rights, which equal law must protect, and to violate would be oppression. Let us, then, fellow-citizens, unite with one heart and one mind. Let us restore to social intercourse that harmony and affection without which liberty and even life itself are but dreary things. And let us reflect that, having banished from our land that religious intolerance under which mankind so long bled and suffered, we have yet gained little if we countenance a political intolerance as despotic, as wicked, and capable of as bitter and bloody persecutions. During the throes and convulsions of the ancient world, during the agonizing spasms of infuriated man, seeking through blood and slaughter his long-lost liberty, it was not wonderful that the agitation of the billows should reach even this distant and peaceful shore; that this should be more felt and feared by some and less by others, and should divide opinions as to measures of safety. But every difference of opinion is not a difference of principle. We have called by different names brethren of the same principle. We are all Republicans, we are all Federalists. If there be any among us who would wish to dissolve this Union or to change its republican form, let them stand undisturbed as monuments of the safety with which error of opinion may be tolerated where reason is left free to combat it. I know, indeed, that some honest men fear that a republican government cannot be strong, that this Government is not strong enough; but would the honest patriot, in the full tide of successful experiment, abandon a government which has so far kept us free and firm on the theoretic and visionary fear that this Government, the world's best hope, may by possibility want energy to preserve itself? I trust not. I believe this, on the contrary, the strongest Government on earth. I believe it the only one where every man, at the call of the law, would fly to the standard of the law, and would meet invasions of the public order as his own personal concern. Sometimes it is said that man cannot be trusted with the government of himself. Can he, then, be trusted with the government of others? Or have we found angels in the forms of kings to govern him? Let history answer this question.

Let us, then, with courage and confidence pursue our own Federal and Republican principles, our attachment to union and representative government. Kindly separated by nature and a wide ocean from the exterminating havoc of one quarter of the globe; too high-minded to endure the degradations of the others; possessing a chosen country, with room enough for our descendants to the thousandth and thousandth generation; entertaining a due sense of our equal right to the use of our own faculties, to the acquisitions of our own industry, to honor and confidence from our fellow-citizens, resulting not from birth, but from our actions and their sense of them; enlightened by a benign religion, professed, indeed, and practiced in various forms, yet all of them inculcating honesty, truth, temperance, gratitude, and the love of man; acknowledging and adoring an overruling Providence, which by all its dispensations proves that it delights in the happiness of man here and his greater happiness hereafter -- with all these blessings, what more is necessary to make us a happy and a prosperous people? Still one thing more, fellow-citizens -- a wise and frugal Government, which shall restrain men from injuring one another, shall leave them otherwise free to regulate their own pursuits of industry and improvement, and shall not take from the mouth of labor the bread it has earned. This is the sum of good government, and this is necessary to close the circle of our felicities.

About to enter, fellow-citizens, on the exercise of duties which comprehend everything dear and valuable to you, it is proper you should understand what I deem the essential principles of our Government, and consequently those which ought to shape its Administration. I will compress them within the narrowest compass they will bear, stating the general principle, but not all its limitations. Equal and exact justice to all men, of whatever state or persuasion, religious or political; peace, commerce, and honest friendship with all nations, entangling alliances with none; the support of the State governments in all their rights, as the most competent administrations for our domestic concerns and the surest bulwarks against anti-republican tendencies; the preservation of the General Government in its whole constitutional vigor, as the sheet anchor of our peace at home and safety abroad; a jealous care of the right of election by the people -- a mild and safe corrective of abuses which are lopped by the sword of revolution where peaceable remedies are unprovided; absolute acquiescence in the decisions of the majority, the vital principle of republics, from which is no appeal but to force, the vital principle and immediate parent of despotism; a well-disciplined militia, our best reliance in peace and for the first moments of war till regulars may relieve them; the supremacy of the civil over the military authority; economy in the public expense, that labor may be lightly burdened; the honest payment of our debts and sacred preservation of the public faith; encouragement of agriculture, and of commerce as its handmaid; the diffusion of information and arraignment of all abuses at the bar of the public reason; freedom of religion; freedom of the press, and freedom of person under the protection of the habeas corpus, and trial by juries impartially selected. These principles form the bright constellation which has gone before us and guided our steps through an age of revolution and reformation. The wisdom of our sages and blood of our heroes have been devoted to their attainment. They should be the creed of our political faith, the text of civic instruction, the touchstone by which to try the services of those we trust; and should we wander from them in moments of error or of alarm, let us hasten to retrace our steps and to regain the road which alone leads to peace, liberty, and safety.

I repair, then, fellow-citizens, to the post you have assigned me. With experience enough in subordinate offices to have seen the difficulties of this the greatest of all, I have learnt to expect that it will rarely fall to the lot of imperfect man to retire from this station with the reputation and the favor which bring him into it. Without pretensions to that high confidence you reposed in our first and greatest revolutionary character, whose preeminent services had entitled him to the first place in his country's love and destined for him the fairest page in the volume of faithful history, I ask so much confidence only as may give firmness and effect to the legal administration of your affairs. I shall often go wrong through defect of judgment. When right, I shall often be thought wrong by those whose positions will not command a view of the whole ground. I ask your indulgence for my own errors, which will never be intentional, and your support against the errors of others, who may condemn what they would not if seen in all its parts. The approbation implied by your suffrage is a great consolation to me for the past, and my future solicitude will be to retain the good opinion of those who have bestowed it in advance, to conciliate that of others by doing them all the good in my power, and to be instrumental to the happiness and freedom of all.

Relying, then, on the patronage of your good will, I advance with obedience to the work, ready to retire from it whenever you become *sensible how much better choice it is in your power to make. And may that Infinite Power which rules the destinies of the universe lead our councils to what is best, and give them a favorable issue for your peace and prosperity.*

Thomas Jefferson

Moderator's Notes: If you remember nothing else from what you just read, remember this gem of indispensable political counsel from Jefferson: "a wise and frugal government, which shall restrain men from injuring one another, shall leave them otherwise free to regulate their own pursuits of industry and improvement, and shall not take from the mouth of labor the bread it has earned. This is the sum of good government; and this is necessary to close the circle of our felicities [happiness]."

GETTYSBURG ADDRESS
(Procured with gratitude from the Lillian Goldman Law Library)

"Fourscore and seven years ago our fathers brought forth on this continent a new nation, conceived in liberty and dedicated to the proposition that all men are created equal. Now we are engaged in a great civil war, testing whether that nation or any nation so conceived and so dedicated can long endure. We are met on a great battlefield of that war. We have come to dedicate a portion of that field as a final resting-place for those who here gave their lives that that nation might live. It is altogether fitting and proper that we should do this. But in a larger sense, we cannot dedicate, we cannot consecrate, we cannot hallow this ground. The brave men, living and dead who struggled here have consecrated it far above our poor power to add or detract. The world will little note nor long remember what we say here, but it can never forget what they did here. It is for us the living rather to be dedicated here to the unfinished work which they who fought here have thus far so nobly advanced. It is rather for us to be here dedicated to the great task remaining before us--that from these honored dead we take increased devotion to that cause for which they gave the last full measure of devotion--that we here highly resolve that these dead shall not have died in vain, that this nation under God shall have a new birth of freedom, and that government of the people, by the people, for the people shall not perish from the earth.

Abraham Lincoln

Moderator's Notes: President Abraham Lincoln gave the Gettysburg Address on the 19th of November, 1863, during the dedication ceremony for the Soldiers' National Cemetery in Gettysburg, Pennsylvania. Former US Congressman and Governor of Massachusetts, the Honorable Edward Everett, gave a two hour speech before Lincoln spoke. Lincoln's address lasted just a few minutes. And yet, it is Lincoln's words, not Everett's, that are firmly anchored in the core of American values and history.

To closeout our time together, I will recall to all Americans, and especially our politicians, Lincoln's profound advice to his fellow citizens at the end of the American Civil War – and as we reach the end of the post 9/11 wars, Lincoln's advice remains more relevant than ever.

"With malice toward none, with charity for all, with firmness in the right as God gives us to see the right, let us strive on to finish the work we are in, to bind up the nation's wounds, to care for him who shall have borne the battle and for his widow and his orphan, to do all which may achieve and cherish a just and lasting peace among ourselves and with all nations." Abraham Lincoln

"Il faut cultiver notre jardin."
(It is necessary to cultivate our own garden).[23]
Voltaire, 18th century French author, from his play, *Candide*

READER'S NOTES

---

[23]   Start with your own garden – your household. Then, move on to your street, your neighborhood, and your town. As Jefferson said, local needs are best handled by local people in conjunction with their local government.

and they've fought for many others' freedom

ABOUT THE AUTHOR

Justin American is just an American. He was born on the eastern edge of the American Midwest, in a small town next to a big town. He enjoyed playing sports, and sang in his high school's annual musical. He went to his prom, said goodbye to his friends, and headed off to become a member of the US armed forces. He owns a beautiful dog, loves and cherishes his wife and his kids, loves his country, and most of all, loves his God. Justin's military service inspired him to learn more about what it really means to "support and defend the Constitution," the oath he took upon entry into the US military. Now, Justin has decided to dedicate the rest of his life to teaching his fellow Americans, and those who aspire to become Americans, what the Founding Fathers meant by Washington's statement: "Citizens by birth or choice, of a common country, that country [USA] has a right to concentrate your affections. The name of American, which belongs to you, in your national capacity, must always exalt the just pride of patriotism, more than any appellation derived from local discriminations."

Made in the USA
Columbia, SC
30 May 2018